LEADERSHIP 180

Daily Meditations
on School Leadership

DENNIS SPARKS

Solution Tree | Press

a division of
Solution Tree

555 North Morton Street

Bloomington, IN 47404

800.733.6786 (toll free) / 812.336.7700

FAX: 812.336.7790

email: info@solution-tree.com

solution-tree.com

Printed in the United States of America

14   13   12   11   10   1   2   3   4   5

FSC

Mixed Sources

Product group from well-managed forests and other controlled sources

Cert no. SW-COC-002283
www.fsc.org
© 1996 Forest Stewardship Council

Library of Congress Cataloging-in-Publication Data

Sparks, Dennis.

Leadership 180 : daily meditations on school leadership / Dennis Sparks.

p. cm.

Includes bibliographical references and index.

ISBN 978-1-935249-82-5 (perfect bound) -- ISBN 978-1-935249-83-2 (library bound) 1. Educational leadership--United States. 2. School management and organization--United States. 3. Educational change--United States. 4. School principals--United States. 5. Education and state--United States. I. Title.

LB2805.S7347 2010

371.2--dc22

2010004636

....

Solution Tree

Jeffrey C. Jones, CEO & President

Solution Tree Press

President: Douglas M. Rife

Publisher: Robert D. Clouse

Vice President of Production: Gretchen Knapp

Managing Production Editor: Caroline Wise

Proofreader: Sue Kraszewski

Cover and Text Designer: Orlando Angel

Acknowledgments

. . . .

I am deeply grateful to Jody Hoch of the Rush-Henrietta Central School District in New York, who served as a first reader for this book and whose comments and suggestions added immensely to its quality.

I am also grateful to the scores of educators and school systems who, over many years, allowed me to test and refine the ideas and practices you will find here. Their learning and the results they achieved inspired me to write this book.

In addition, I would like to express my appreciation to Solution Tree Press Publisher Robb Clouse for his support of this unconventional book, and to Managing Production Editor Caroline Wise for her careful editing.

Table of Contents

. . . .

About the Author

Dennis Sparks serves as a "thinking partner" to leadership teams of education organizations that are committed to the continuous improvement of teaching and learning for all students. He is emeritus executive director of the National Staff Development Council, having served as its executive director from 1984–2007. Dennis has spoken to numerous educational groups and published on a wide variety of subjects in most major educational publications. His other publications include *Leading for Results: Transforming Teaching, Learning, and Relationships in Schools*, and a blog on school leadership which can be found at http://dennissparks.wordpress.com.

Introduction

. . . .

Welcome to *Leadership 180: Daily Meditations on School Leadership*! I intend *Leadership 180* to make a significant and lasting difference in the practice of your leadership, the quality of your professional life, and the effectiveness of the school community with which you are engaged. This introduction provides a context for and an overview of this book's key features.

The number of essays included in this book was selected to match the 180 days found in the traditional school year. The number 180 also recognizes the possibility of a dramatic change in direction that can occur within leaders and school communities when leaders alter their beliefs, deepen their understanding of key ideas and practices, and develop new habits. Each topic addressed in this book was carefully selected because of its power to influence leaders' understanding and actions in ways that could make profound and permanent improvements in teaching, learning, and relationships in schools.

In recognition of the fast pace and intensity of school leaders' professional lives, the 180 brief essays contained here can be contemplated and actions taken in just a few minutes a day. The "meditations" can be read in any order, and I encourage you to dip into them to suit your interests and the challenges you are facing in your work that day. You will notice a repetition of a few topics as I circle back to them from different directions. These ideas, linked to the following foundational beliefs, are the core leadership practices that enable transformational change that begins with leaders and radiates from them throughout the organization.

I Believe . . .

The inspiration for this book was drawn from "This I Believe," a popular and durable series of essays dating from the 1950s that found expression in newspaper columns, books, a website (www.thisibelieve.org), and a long-running National Public Radio "Morning Edition" series.

A fundamental purpose of *Leadership 180* is expressed by editor Jay Allison in his introduction to *This I Believe: The Personal Philosophies of Remarkable Men and Women* (2007): "Beliefs are choices. No one has authority over your personal beliefs. . . . Understanding your own beliefs, and those of others, comes only through focused thought and discussion" (p. 6). Allison laments that "amid the most pervasive information delivery systems in history, there is little place for the encouragement of quiet listening to the beliefs of others without rebuttal and criticism" (pp. 2–3).

It is essential, I believe, for leaders to continuously clarify their beliefs on a number of important subjects related to leadership, teaching, learning, and relationships in schools. Clarity regarding beliefs is the bedrock that supports important decisions and actions. I want leaders to better understand their own beliefs, and these "meditations" provide a means to achieve the "focused thought and discussion" that Allison advocates.

I offer several beliefs that provide the foundation for many of the ideas and practices that appear in this book. *I believe that:*

- *Beliefs are an incredibly powerful and often overlooked force in shaping practice.* Leaders' mental models or conceptual frames affect their daily actions, which, in turn, have real-world consequences.

- *Clarity is essential, and the larger one's scope of influence, the more important it is.* Clarity is the antidote to the complexity that hides rather than reveals meaning. Deep understanding simply expressed is a key factor in continuous improvement.

- *Culture trumps innovation.* School culture can anchor the status quo or aid in the continuous improvement of teaching and learning.

- *Professional practice is basically a bundle of habits.* Leaders can intentionally develop new habits of mind and behavior to serve new, compelling purposes.

- *A continuous stream of goal-focused actions establishes a sense of urgency and maintains momentum.* Small, carefully selected steps consistently taken can, over time, make a significant difference.

- *Emotions are contagious.* Leaders' emotions—both positive and negative—can spread from person to person, often without a word being spoken.

- *Candor is essential when it serves the well-being of young people.* Honesty about important values and ideas requires clarity about one's viewpoint, and it often requires courage.

- *Purposeful learning adds meaning and vitality to life.* Successful leaders are voracious learners. Such learning is important because leaders' beliefs, understandings, and actions affect the entire school community.

- *Authenticity and integrity matter.* Leaders' authenticity and integrity are potent forces in shaping school culture and enabling continuous improvement.

- *We accomplish more together than we do alone.* Teamwork at all levels is a prerequisite to continuous improvement.

- *The solution to significant educational problems requires innovation as well as adoption of "best practices."* Leaders who unleash an innovative spirit in their school communities tap a powerful force for continuous improvement of teaching and learning.

- *Some things matter a lot more than others.* Leaders who distinguish the trivial from the important and the important from the essential focus their work and that of the school community.

I encourage you to use these beliefs and the meditations as a stimulus to prepare "I believe" essays of your own on subjects particularly important in your work and life. Likewise, I hope these essays encourage you to create school cultures in which, according to Jay Allison, "quiet listening to the beliefs of others without rebuttal or criticism" is the norm.

Today I Will . . .

Each meditation concludes with a "Today I will . . ." activity to encourage immediate application of the ideas or principles they offer. Many of these activities focus readers on a "micro-goal," an action so small and focused that failure is unlikely and whose completion begins to develop new neural networks in the brain (Maurer 2004). The achievement of the micro-goal may also provide the impetus for development of an important new professional habit of mind or behavior.

To a large degree, leaders' efforts to improve teaching, learning, and relationships in schools can be viewed as a continuous stream of tasks—which sometimes may feel like a raging river—whose daily and hourly management and completion are the key to success. When leaders lose track of actions they have promised to take or a project's momentum falters because their attention is diverted, both their integrity and ability to affect the results they most desire are diminished.

"Next-action thinking" focused on achieving clearly defined outcomes is a fundamental leadership discipline that enhances individual and organizational energy and maintains momentum. In *Getting Things Done: The Art of Stress-Free Productivity* (2001), David Allen writes, "Over the years I have noticed an extraordinary shift in energy and productivity whenever individuals and groups installed 'What's the next action?' as a fundamental and consistently asked question" (p. 236). The result, he says, would be that "no meeting or discussion will end, and no interaction cease, without a clear determination of whether or not some action is needed—and if it is, what it will be, or at least who has responsibility for it." Allen argues that "shifting your focus to something that your mind perceives as a doable, completable task will create a real increase in positive energy, direction, and motivation" (p. 242).

While complex projects may benefit from brainstorming and representing information visually using mindmaps or electronic tools, Allen believes that 80 percent of projects can be successfully managed by simply listing their outcomes and the next actions for each using the widely available tools of a pencil and the back of an envelope.

While a continuous stream of work-related actions are essential to leaders' success, I hope that some actions you take as a result of reading this book serve the goal of living a healthier, more balanced life—for instance, spending more time with family, eating better, or exercising regularly. When leaders successfully manage those tasks, they not only improve the quality of their lives, but they demonstrate at the most basic level that they are people who can be counted on to keep their promises, beginning with the promises they make to themselves.

I encourage you to pay close attention to those topics that resonate with you, which may be a sign that those ideas are particularly significant in your work. Likewise, I hope that you pay attention to those subjects about which you have strong negative feelings, another sign of the potential value of those topics for further exploration.

Whether you decide to read this book sequentially from cover to cover, dip into it based on your interest at the moment, or focus on meditations related to a particular theme, I believe that the topics addressed in these pages and the actions I encourage you to take can profoundly influence you as a human being and as a leader, as well as the school community whose success and well-being will be at the center of our attention. That is my goal, and I wish you well in the journey.

References

Allen, D. (2003). *Getting things done: The art of stress-free productivity.* New York: Penguin.

Allison, J., & Gediman, D. (Eds.) (2007). *This I believe: The personal philosophies of remarkable men and women.* New York: Henry Holt and Company.

Maurer, R. (2004). *One small step can change your life: The Kaizen way.* New York: Workman Publishing.

I

Change Yourself First

One key to successful leadership is continuous personal change. Personal change is a reflection of our inner growth and empowerment. Empowered leaders are the only ones who can induce real change.

—*Robert Quinn*

Important, lasting improvements in teaching, learning, and relationships in schools occur when leaders adopt new beliefs, deepen their understanding of important issues, and consistently speak and act in new ways. A common human tendency is to see others' shortcomings before noticing our own complicity in maintaining the status quo. It's also human for leaders to believe that the primary barriers to change reside outside themselves. Leaders who understand these dynamics begin the change process by making significant and deep changes in themselves.

· ·

Today I will reflect on an important school goal to determine a belief I want to modify, an understanding I want to deepen, a skill I would like to acquire, or a habit I want to develop.

2

Learn Forever

Life is like riding a bicycle. To keep your balance you must keep moving.
—*Albert Einstein*

Learning adds vitality and sense of purpose throughout the life span. Leaders' most important learning comes as they pursue important individual and collective goals. They adopt new beliefs, deepen their understanding of important ideas, experiment with new practices, and reflect on what they can learn from those experiences. Such relentless effort is particularly important for school leaders because their learning, purposefulness, and vitality affect the entire school community.

. . . .

Today I will take a few minutes to commit in writing to a professional learning goal that will stretch me and benefit the school community; I will mark dates on my calendar when I will review my progress. To increase my clarity and commitment, I will share the goal with a colleague.

3

Cultivate Head, Heart, and Spirit

A principal's work is of the spirit. We must be convinced that children depend on who we are and what we do.

—*Joanne Rooney*

Leaders affect the head, heart, and spirit of school communities through their own heads, hearts, and spirits. Leaders sometimes underestimate the profound, positive differences they can make in the lives of the adults and young people with whom they interact each day. While leaders' knowledge and technical skills are important, their physical and emotional well-being, integrity, passion, and joy they bring to their responsibilities are also essential elements of their work.

. . . .

Today I will reflect on the positive differences I make in the lives of young people and adults, and I will celebrate all the ways in which I contribute to the school community.

4

Speak With an Authentic Voice

> We grant authority to people we perceive as "authoring" their own words and actions, people who do not speak from a script or behave in preprogrammed ways.
>
> —*Parker Palmer*

A leader's authentic voice is one of his or her most important leadership "tools." Simply put, a leader's voice is a clear and genuine expression of his or her intentions, ideas, beliefs, values, and emotions, a voice brought into every meeting, professional learning setting, and one-to-one interaction with teachers, parents, and students. Leaders have an authentic voice when they speak from their own hearts and values rather than sound as though they are reading from or acting out a script provided by others.

· ·

Today I will reflect on the extent to which what I really think and value on the inside is expressed to the outside world through my words and actions. I will identify ways to reduce any discrepancies I may find.

5

Distinguish Degrees of Importance

A life is made simple by adopting the principle of hierarchy. Life is very complex when we make everything equal. . . . When we begin to sort out what's more important and what's less important, we begin to sort out the complexity.

—*Robert Fritz*

Leaders' ability to discriminate between what is more important and less important is essential in achieving the school community's most important goals. While it's essential that leaders separate the important from the unimportant, it's even more critical that they can make distinctions between the essential and the merely worthwhile. Making distinctions, of course, is a matter of judgment, and leaders continuously refine their professional judgment when they reflect on the effectiveness of their previous decisions and actions and apply what they learned in new situations.

• •

Today I will select an aspect of my work that I believe is essential in improving teaching, learning, and relationships in the school community and I will commit to taking an action that will further that purpose.

6

Have Simple, Clear Plans

There is evidence that schools are well served by one-page plans that are clearly focused and simple enough that every participant in the process understand his or her role in executing the plan.

—Douglas Reeves

Leaders' clarity about goals and the methods the school community will employ for their achievement is essential to the success of school improvement plans. The realization of important district and school outcomes depends on leaders' abilities to articulate those goals in clear and compelling language and describe the actions they and others will take to achieve them. In turn, leaders ask those with whom they work to describe in clear, concrete language the outcomes they will pursue and the actions they will take that fit their unique roles and responsibilities.

. . . .

Today I will take a moment to express in simple, everyday terms an important outcome and the next action I and others will take to achieve it. I will check my clarity by describing the plan to others and asking them to paraphrase it in their own words.

7

Act on Your Values

> I'd like to suggest to you, just in case you haven't done it lately, that this
> would be a good time to find out what your values are, and then figure
> out how you're going to be able to live by them. Knowing what you are
> about and then devoting yourself to it is just about the only way you're
> going to be able to have a sense of purpose in your life.
>
> *—Alan Alda*

Leaders' values are the touchstone of their most important decisions and
actions. Leaders who know what is important to them and to their school
communities can provide consistency of purpose across the months and
years that significant improvements require. Because what is important
evolves based on life experience and learning, effective leaders periodically
assess and affirm their bedrock values.

• • • • • • • • • • • • • • • • • • • •

Today I will list my five most important personal values and five most
important professional values and determine an action I will take today in
support of one or more of those values.

8

Have Integrity

> Only one thing is more toxic and destructive than a promise made and not kept: a pattern of promises made and not kept.
>
> —*Roland Barth*

Leaders' integrity is their most important leadership attribute. Leaders demonstrate integrity when they align their actions with their values, match their actions with their words, and keep their promises. Their integrity is also measured by honesty in forthrightly expressing their views on important issues. Such integrity enables members of the school community to trust their leaders, which, in turn, affects the level of trust felt throughout the community.

. . . .

Today I will carefully consider whether my words and actions match my values, whether I fulfill my promises, and whether I speak with candor on important subjects.

9

Engage in Team-Based Learning

Principals need opportunities to collaborate with their peers in the type of learning they will use to lead their schools toward increased student achievement.

—*Hayes Mizell*

When leaders engage in team-based professional learning with other leaders as a means of continuous improvement, they develop an understanding that can be acquired only through direct experience of why teamwork is critically important for teachers in their schools. Leaders truly appreciate the power of professional communities to alter beliefs, deepen understanding, and change daily practice when they pursue with their colleagues stretching, worthy goals that cannot be achieved through independent action. Also, leaders acquire knowledge and skills that help them solve significant problems.

• •

Today I will identify one or more colleagues to join me in a project that will require new learning on our parts for its successful completion. The project might be as limited as designing an agenda for a faculty meeting whose primary purpose is to create productive discussion among teachers about an important schoolwide issue, or as complex as creating meaningful professional learning communities in the school that affect every teacher and benefit all students.

10

Find the Simplicity Beyond Complexity

Great leaders are almost always great simplifiers.

—*Colin Powell*

Simplicity and clarity are essential leadership tools. As leaders learn about new ideas and practices, their understanding naturally becomes more elaborate and nuanced. Sometimes, however, the complexity such understanding can produce becomes a barrier to effective communication. When leaders pursue the clarity that resides beyond the complexity, they find simple, everyday words, examples, and stories that enable them to explain their ideas with proverb-like clarity.

. . . .

Today I will take a few minutes to practice expressing a complex idea in simple terms. For example, "*Professional community* means that we support each other every day in finding practical ways to improve the learning of all our students to agreed-on standards. We will do that in our grade-level meetings and faculty meetings and during professional development sessions."

II

Be Clear About Your Vision

Clarity and focus describe the most basic predispositions of authentic leaders: they know what they want, and they pursue it.

—*Robert Evans*

Leaders' effectiveness is determined by the clarity of their vision of a desired future for the school community and of the next steps they and others will take to realize it. Such clarity is most influential when it is a product of consensus seeking and learning throughout the community. Leaders—and others in the school community—demonstrate clarity through their ability to succinctly express the core elements of important ideas. They also show clarity by telling stories that touch hearts and minds and that illustrate with concrete details those ideas enacted in the daily lives of the school.

. . . .

Today I will take a moment to describe in writing a compelling image I and others have for the school (providing as much detail as possible) and the next steps we will take to manifest that vision.

I2

Write to Learn

> I thought of how often as a writer I had made clear to myself some subject I had previously known nothing about by just putting one sentence after another—by reasoning my way in sequential steps to its meaning. I thought of how often the act of writing even the simplest document— a letter, for instance—has clarified my half-formed ideas. Writing and thinking and learning were the same process.
>
> —*William Zinsser*

Writing is a potent and underused learning tool that leaders can use to acquire a deeper understanding of important subjects and to give shape to their ideas. Because writing is frozen thought, it enables leaders to examine the clarity and logical consistency of their thinking and reveals areas for further exploration and learning. Writing can also help busy leaders separate the essential from the nonessential.

. . . .

Today I will use writing to teach myself about a subject of importance and to clarify the next actions I may take related to that subject.

13

Nurture the Soul

> Growing our souls could be defined as the steady accretion of empathy, clarity, and passion for the good.
>
> —*Mary Pipher*

Wise leaders nurture their own souls and the soul of the school community. Individuals and schools with soul are typically experienced as authentic, profound, personally meaningful, and emotionally stirring. Leaders who nourish their own interior lives are more likely to display the generosity of spirit, empathy, and profound respect for others that call forth the soul of the organization.

· ·

Today I will attend to my interior life as a first step in honoring and encouraging the expression of the unique personhood of all those with whom I interact.

14

Make Difficult Decisions

I cannot give you the formula for success, but I can give you the formula of failure—which is try to please everybody.

—Herbert B. Swope

One of leaders' most important responsibilities is making difficult decisions on behalf of the school community. Their clarity of purpose and courage are tested in such situations because someone will almost certainly be dissatisfied with the decision. When leaders try to please everyone, hard decisions that affect the well-being of individuals or community are avoided and progress is stalled. When faced with such decisions, leaders must clarify their most important purposes, values, and ideas—and those of the school community—to explain their viewpoint and to inspire courage.

* *

Today I will identify a decision I have been avoiding and determine which purposes, values, and ideas are relevant to the decision. Because it is not necessary to tackle the most difficult decisions first, I will start with one whose resolution will inspire me to tackle larger issues.

15

View Everyone as Teacher and Student

In our family, we have a motto: you are not too old too learn, and you are not too young to teach.

> —*Immigrant father remarking on the simultaneous college graduation of several family members*

Students and adults thrive in schools in which learning flows in all directions, no matter one's role or age. In such schools the oldest learns from youngest, students learn from their teachers and from each other, and adults continuously learn from each other and their students. While the lessons are sometimes planned and structured, they are often informal as insights and joy spontaneously spread in many directions throughout the school community.

. . . .

Today I will recall a time I learned an important lesson from a student or colleague and determine a time when I can share that lesson with others in the school community. I will invite others in turn to share similar stories with me.

16

Remember Your Fundamental Purpose

Sensibilities such as love, engaging with intellectual work, the hope of changing students' lives, a belief in the democratic potential of public education, and anger at the conditions of public education are all the heart of what makes for excellent and caring teachers.

—Sonia Nieto

Leaders' most fundamental purposes are the touchstones that provide guidance and motivation throughout their careers. Sometimes, however, leaders lose touch with those purposes as day-to-day responsibilities consume larger portions of their attention. Examples of such purposes include the desire to improve the lives of children, to share the joy of curiosity and learning, and to ensure the future viability of our democratic form of government. By keeping their fundamental purposes at the forefront of their work, leaders can better maintain their focus and tap an ever-present source of energy throughout their careers.

· ·

Today I will remind myself why I am an educator and of the motivations that led me to assume leadership responsibilities. I will post that purpose in my calendar or on a bulletin board to focus and energize my work.

17

Choose to Dance

And when you get the choice to sit it out or dance, I hope you dance.
—Mark D. Sanders & Tia Sillers

Leaders who engage deeply with life bring a joy and enthusiasm to their work that spreads throughout the school community. Because leaders' emotions are infectious, their ability to cultivate positive emotions in themselves benefits the students, teachers, and family members with whom they interact each day. Such leaders are aware of the moments when they are most deeply engaged and flowing in the expression of their interests and talents, and they cultivate those moments in themselves and others.

Today I will recall times when I felt most alive and engaged. I will identify ways I can increase the frequency of such events and savor the joy they bring me in the knowledge that my joy through its very presence will infect others around me.

18

Create Cultures That Enable New Practices

Practice changes not so much from new ideas as from changes in the way work is organized and in the culture of organizations and professions.

—Ben Levin

One important responsibility of leaders is to cocreate with other members of their school communities cultures of trust, collaboration, and continuous improvement. These cultures promote teamwork and sustained, productive professional conversations about values, ideas, and methods for improvement. They also enable candid and respectful discussions about problems and their solutions. In addition, such cultures promote the sharing of successful practices that already exist within the school but may be unknown to others because traditional organizational structures promote professional isolation.

• •

Today I will choose a conversation or meeting in which I will invite others to share an example of a cultural attribute such as trust, interpersonal accountability, or respect that they believe is important to cultivate in our community. In turn, I will offer an example of an attribute that I value.

19

Cultivate Empathy

Empathy is the key to all relationships.

—Garret FitzGerald

A leader's ability to understand how others view the world is essential to the development of positive relationships. Accurately determining others' perspectives and communicating respect for their views is a hallmark of emotional intelligence and the foundation of a productive work environment. The cultivation of empathy acknowledges that people of good will often possess alternative perspectives, which in turn enrich and benefit the school community.

. . . .

Today I will demonstrate to someone that I hear, understand, and respect his or her views.

20

Establish Ambitious Goals

You must undertake something so great that you cannot accomplish it unaided.

—Phillip Brooks

Ambitious goals are more likely than modest goals to produce significant and lasting improvements in teaching and learning in all classrooms. The achievement of stretch goals requires deep change in an interconnected system of beliefs, curriculum, assessment, and pedagogy. By their very nature, such goals also require teamwork because they cannot be achieved by an individual working alone. Of course, establishing a stretch goal demands courage because the natural human tendency is to set modest goals that ensure success. However, without the establishment of at least one worthy stretch goal, the school community never fully knows what it can accomplish.

. . . .

Today I will select an area in which a stretching goal for myself or the school community would be desirable. I will commit the goal to writing and continue to develop clarity by sharing it with at least one other person.

21

Appreciate and Celebrate

The deepest principle of human nature is the craving to be appreciated.
—*William James*

Leaders increase motivation and commitment to long-term purposes when they express appreciation and celebrate progress. Through their actions, effective leaders acknowledge individuals' contributions and draw attention to the school community's incremental progress toward important goals. Over time, these celebrations become embedded in the school culture and energize students, teachers, and parents.

. . . .

Today I will reflect on the current status of appreciation and celebration as central features of our school culture and determine ways these qualities may be enhanced.

22

Pay Attention and Remain Open

And if I had to think about wisdom I could impart . . . I would say pay
attention. . . . Pay attention, listen, and keep an open mind.

—*Robert Redford*

A leader's ability to be fully present and open to what can be learned in
every situation promotes a receptive climate to change that affects the
entire school community. Because leaders' personal and professional lives
are filled to the brim with activities, and because our society mistakenly
promotes multitasking as a productivity tool, being attentive and open to
what is in front of us can be challenging. Nonetheless, moment-to-moment
awareness is essential in developing strong relationships, maintaining a
focus on priorities, and deepening professional learning.

* *

Today I will choose an activity or event during which I will strive to be
fully present, if even for just a moment or two. If I find my mind wandering,
I will gently bring it back to the task at hand.

23

Ensure Teacher-to-Teacher Learning

A player-coached team is better than a coach-coached team.
—*Tom Izzo*

Teacher-to-teacher professional learning embedded with ongoing teams is an essential means of continuous improvement. All students benefit when teachers deepen each other's understanding of curriculum, pedagogy, and assessment. Such learning typically (but not exclusively) occurs during team meetings or other conversations focused on helping all students within the teachers' charge meet agreed-on standards.

. . . .

Today I will assess the quality of teacher-to-teacher learning that occurs within the school by attending meetings, reviewing meeting logs, examining the products of team meetings, and visiting classrooms to assess the implementation of learning. I will then determine a next action to strengthen the breadth and depth of this learning.

24

Serve Students Through Values-Guided Leadership

> We must learn to distinguish between what is "merely important" and what is "wildly important."
>
> —*Stephen Covey*

Leaders who positively impact the lives of youngsters understand their values and consult them to guide what they think, say, and do. Each day district administrators, principals, and teacher leaders face critically important values-laden decisions regarding resource allocation, curriculum, pedagogy, and school culture. Because taking a stand may put leaders at risk of criticism, ostracism, or even more dire consequences, their awareness of the values that guide them can inspire courage in the face of their fears.

• • • • • • • • • • • • • • • • • • • •

Today I will take a few minutes to reflect on what's most important to me and how those values can be best expressed in my life.

25

Make Professional Learning Part of the School Day

> We must make professional learning an everyday experience for all educators.
>
> —*Michael Fullan*

The most valuable forms of professional learning occur among teachers as they engage in the core responsibilities of their work. This learning occurs as teachers work together to plan lessons, analyze data and other forms of evidence, and pursue solutions to classroom and schoolwide problems. Teachers' learning is not an add-on to their workday; it is a fundamental part of it.

. . . .

Today I will talk with a colleague about the strengths and weaknesses of our professional learning efforts and take a few minutes to read an article to identify ways to more effectively embed learning in teachers' day-to-day responsibilities. (The website of the National Staff Development Council, www.nsdc.org, provides useful resources.)

26

Envision the Future

> Talent is like the marksman who hits a target which others cannot reach; genius is like the marksman who hits a target, as far as which others cannot even see.
>
> *—Arthur Schopenhauer*

Effective leaders visualize a stretching, compelling future for the school community and relentlessly pursue it with that community until it is realized. Creation begins in the human imagination as leaders and others see in their mind's eye a future that expresses their most important values, purposes, and ideas. They then describe that image in sufficiently rich detail to enable others to visualize it. This collective vision then becomes an extraordinarily powerful force in creating a desired future.

· ·

Today I will describe in as much detail as possible one or more elements—teaching, assessment, relationships between adults and students, and so on—of my vision for the school community. I will commit my vision to writing, share it with others, and ask them to contribute to it.

27

Tell Our Truth

> Instead of withholding our thoughts and feelings, we can share them.
> We can tell the truth—not *The Truth* (as in assuming our ideas are always
> right) but *our* truth, the way we honestly think and feel. . . . Refusing
> to speak our minds often cheats others of an opportunity to look at a
> problem with a fresh pair of eyes.
>
> —*Dave Ellis*

Leaders' candor in describing current reality as they perceive it is a catalyst
to continuous improvement in teaching and learning. Members of some
school communities find it difficult to have honest discussions related to
differences in performance among student subgroups and ways all students
can be helped to succeed. In those communities, leaders must respectfully,
relentlessly, and sometimes courageously offer their unique schoolwide
perspectives to perturb the status quo and point the direction for significant
improvements.

• •

Today I will identify an aspect of current reality that I think is important for the school community to address. As a first step in airing it in the
spirit of dialogue, I will draft my thoughts on the subject to ensure that
my language is respectful, solution-oriented, and focused on the future
rather than the past.

28

View Mistakes as Our Teachers

> I always say that there's no mistake if you can resolve it, whether it's in your music or in your life. Sometimes the mistake motivates you or elevates you into a different circumstance that can be better.
>
> —*Dave Brubeck*

Mistakes can be important teachers, particularly the kind that leaders are likely to make as they intentionally stretch themselves to higher performance levels. Although mistakes are inevitable, leaders determine how they view them and what they learn because of them. The same is true for others' mistakes. Rather than assess blame, effective leaders encourage those with whom they work to learn from their experiences and to apply that learning in future situations.

. . . .

Today I will identify a mistake that I recently made, determine what I have learned from it, and in the spirit of openness tell those most affected by it about my learning. Such candor will encourage others to accept and learn from their own mistakes and those of others.

29

Promote Laughter

Laughter is wine for the soul—laugh soft, or loud and deep, tinged through with seriousness. Comedy and tragedy step through life together, arm in arm. . . . Once we can laugh, we can live.

—*Sean O'Casey*

The ability to laugh and to express humor in uplifting ways contributes to leaders' own emotional well-being and that of the school community. Unlike humor that diminishes and separates, uplifting humor enriches the spirit and draws people together. Fortunately, school settings and interactions with young people can be a daily source of joy and laughter when leaders are attuned to those moments.

. . . .

Today I will pay attention to the lightness and humor that students and colleagues bring into my life and will look for appropriate times to share those moments with others.

30

Create Authentic Teams

Authentic teams build effective curriculum-based lessons and units together—which they routinely refine together on the basis of common
assessment data.

—Mike Schmoker

Authentic teams have goals large enough that they require interdependent
action and agreements about how individuals will work together to improve
productivity and strengthen relationships. The stretching goals and group
agreements build trust, create positive energy, provide clarity regarding
next steps, and promote accountability among team members. The synergy
and mutual support provided by authentic teams enables schools to achieve
ambitious goals for the learning of all students.

* *

Today I will determine whether the teams of which I am a member and
those I supervise have stretching goals that require interdependence and
group agreements that promote mutual accountability and positive energy.

3I

Have a Plan

Having a plan, even if it's imperfect, will make you much better off.
—*Chris Crowley*

The most powerful plans are often very simple ones that describe a goal and the next actions that will be taken to achieve it. However, more complex planning processes are also useful because they enable school communities to determine their most important long-term strategic purposes and to more rapidly recognize emerging opportunities that will further those purposes. Strong plans, therefore, embody both a long-term, organizational-stretching perspective and an improvisational spirit that enable the plans to adapt to new circumstances and to learning that occurs as the plans are being implemented.

. . . .

Today I will sketch a simple "back-of-the-envelope" plan that furthers a long-term strategic purpose.

32

Encourage Risk Taking and Experimentation

The only man who never makes a mistake is the man who never does anything.

—*Theodore Roosevelt*

Well-considered risk taking is an essential element of both individual and community growth. Leaders encourage ceaseless results-oriented experimentation as a means of achieving important goals. Experiments that lead to improvements in learning and relationships are integrated into a school's practices, and those that do not are followed by new experiments.

. . . .

Today I will assess both my own tolerance and that of the school community for risk taking and experimentation. I will identify a next action to advance the presence of these qualities in the school's culture.

33

Increase Positive Interactions

If you want to build a supportive relationship, you need to give the other person in the relationship at least six positive comments for every negative one.

—Thomas R. Hoerr

Intentionally increasing the number of positive interactions with members of the school community can transform relationships and improve school culture. It's important to remember to establish a high ratio of positive to negative statements. Such a ratio establishes an "emotional bank account" that provides reserves for the important but difficult conversations that are often part of valued relationships.

. . . .

Today I will tally the number of positive and negative comments I make to others in the school community. Building on this assessment, I will increase my awareness of situations worthy of positive comment and be certain to express my feelings about them.

34

Go Together

If you want to go quickly, go alone; if you want to go far, go together.
—African proverb

The goal of quality learning for every student every day requires that school communities move forward together. Such interdependent progress is founded on a stretching, compelling purpose and is supported by school schedules that provide teachers with regular professional planning and learning time. Leaders maintain focus by using schools' long-term visions and the intermediate steps that will take them there to provide both a sense of urgency and a way to measure and mark the small wins required to maintain momentum.

. . . .

Today I will reflect on the extent to which the school is using genuine teamwork to focus on its long-term vision and to achieve the intermediate goals whose accomplishment maintains a sense of momentum. If appropriate, I will schedule a time when the community can celebrate one or more small wins.

35

Promote Deep and Sustained Professional Conversations

As mentor teachers with the New Teacher Center, we worked with teachers who noticed that their students lacked the skills they needed to focus, deepen, and extend conversations about academic topics.

—*Jeff Zwiers & Marie Crawford*

Students are more likely to acquire deep understanding of important subjects when their teachers acquire deep understanding of important assumptions and ideas as part of their professional lives. Teachers who do not experience substantial conversation-based learning as part of their professional lives are less likely to value it for their students. For such professional learning to occur among educators, leaders must value it and set aside generous amounts of time for sustained, focused conversations in faculty and team meetings.

· · · · · · · · · · · · · · · · · · · ·

Today I will select an important assumption or idea that requires deep, sustained conversation and schedule time for it during upcoming meetings.

36

Make Reading and Writing Core Professional Activities

> [W]e believe that nothing replaces the unique contributions of print literacy for the development of the full panoply of the slower, constructive, cognitive processes that invite children to create their own whole worlds in what Proust called the "reading sanctuary."
>
> —*Maryanne Wolf & Mirit Barzillai*

Students are far more likely to engage in "slower, constructive, cognitive processes" in schools in which educators understand the value of such processes because they engage in them as part of their professional responsibilities. "Close reading" with pen in hand and writing to learn promote deeper understanding and the acquisition of meaning in both students and educators alike. The inclusion of professional reading and writing as regular features of faculty and other community meetings is central to sustained learning and to continuous improvement in teaching and learning for all students.

• •

Today I will take a few minutes to closely read a text that is important to me—an article from a professional journal, a book chapter, or even a poem. I will engage with the text by making marginal notes and writing a few sentences regarding my views on the subject.

37

Be Persistent and Patient in Creating New Cultures

> The ultimate solution . . . is to create the right culture. . . . Always treat new cultures as fragile, where a single action . . . can hurt greatly. Be patient, because it takes time for new behaviors to sink in and become organizational norms based on supporting shared values.
>
> *—John Kotter*

Persistence and patience are essential in creating high-performing school cultures. Because cultures are for the most part a bundle of long-standing habits, successful leaders provide frequent opportunities for members of the school community to learn and practice new habits of mind and behavior. Through sustained conversation and repetition—often far more repetition than leaders may initially think necessary—the school cultivates trust, interpersonal accountability, and an ethos of continuous improvement.

. . . .

Today I will consider the school community's progress to date on its journey toward a high-performance culture and determine the next steps I will take to sustain its momentum.

38

Use External Partners to Maintain Momentum

The external partner became a vital source for keeping the momentum going. . . . One of the challenges in systemic change is remaining focused, because there are so many competing commitments.

—*Eileen Howley*

Leadership for continuous improvement requires discipline in maintaining focus and momentum in the face of many distractions. Successful leaders learn to separate the trivial from the important and to further distinguish between the important and the essential. To that end, these leaders regularly engage with external and internal networks and other sources of expertise to reflect on their current work, celebrate success, and determine next actions.

• •

Today I will consider ways in which I can initiate or strengthen internal and external networks to help me maintain focus and to offer hope and sustain high energy levels.

39

Be Intentional About Habits

We are what we repeatedly do. Excellence, then, is not an act, but a habit.
—*Aristotle*

Leaders' habits—their sometimes unconscious "default settings"—can impede or support continuous improvement efforts. When effective leaders become aware of ineffective habits, they purposefully develop new habits of mind and behavior that better serve themselves and their school communities. These new habits begin with intention and become their new default settings through repetition over many months of practice.

• • • • • • • • • • • • • • • • • • •

Today I will pick a new habit I would like to develop to improve my effectiveness and will use my calendar or to-do list to remind myself to practice it daily. At the end of each day, I will assess my progress by noting my use of the new thought or behavior.

40

Act Your Way Into New Beliefs

There is abundant evidence in the fields of psychology, organizational development, and education that changes in attitudes follow rather than precede changes in behavior. When work is designed to require people to act in new ways, the possibility of new experiences are created for them. If those new experiences are positive, they can lead to new attitudes and assumptions over time.

—*Richard DuFour*

Educators are as likely to act themselves into new ways of thinking as they are to think their way into new ways of acting. When leaders design structures that support genuine teamwork among teachers and promote interpersonal accountability for improved student learning, many teachers may for the first time engage in professional, results-oriented conversations that commit them to implementing new practices. Teachers' attitudes and beliefs about students' ability to learn are likely to shift as they experience success from experimentation with approaches acquired from their peers or through other professional learning processes.

* *

Today I will identify an attitude or belief that I would like to develop in support of an important goal (for instance, the belief that solutions to important problems can be found within the school rather than imported through the use of outside experts) and consider what experiences might enable that new way of thinking (for instance, visiting a school with similar student demographics whose structures and culture support the internal sharing of effective practices).

41

Make Professional Learning a Core Leadership Responsibility

Professional development is the centerpiece of administering a district committed to continuous improvement in student learning.

—*Elaine Fink & Lauren B. Resnick*

In schools it is everyone's job to learn. Consequently, nothing can substitute for leaders' active engagement in their organizations' learning agenda, which includes the development of young people and adults alike. The starting place for that agenda is leaders' own learning that is sufficiently robust to produce significant changes in their own beliefs, understanding, and actions.

· · · · · · · · · · · · · · · · · · ·

Today I will identify an area for my own learning that is crucial to the continuous improvement of teaching and learning in my setting and determine the next step in the learning process.

42

Link Learning to Real Work

Undergraduates learn most when they're asked to solve problems, perform original research, work collaboratively—and receive regular feedback from the professor and their peers. The passive, impersonal lecture turned out to be the worst of all possible worlds.

—Kevin Carey

Learners of all ages benefit when they are engaged in real work that generates new knowledge and skills rather than serve as passive recipients of others' intellectual work. Whenever possible, learners identify and weigh alternative solutions to problems they face each day in their lives, write to communicate their views and to promote learning in themselves and others, and participate in deep, sustained conversations about issues of importance to them. Those principles apply to "students" of all ages, including both the young people and adults in K–12 settings.

• • • • • • • • • • • • • • • • • • • •

Today I will select an area in which teachers' deep understanding and weighing of alternatives is essential to the solution of an important problem and determine a next action for promoting that engagement.

43

Determine the Focus for Your Instructional Leadership

> A principal . . . can . . . create an organization that is continuously developing the social capital that allows people to trust, depend on, and learn from each other. But an effective instructional leader also needs to build intellectual capital—by playing a substantive role in curriculum choices, in establishing expectations for the quality of student work, in analyzing the form and quality of teaching, and in organizing targeted opportunities for teachers in the school to learn the specifics of teaching their subject matters well.
>
> —*Elaine Fink & Lauren B. Resnick*

Leaders' first and foremost responsibility is the continuous improvement of teaching and learning for the benefit of all students. This responsibility includes creating cultures that nurture strong professional relationships. It means providing intellectual leadership in curriculum, teaching, and assessment and being able to explain succinctly and precisely in everyday language the key ideas and strategies that guide improvement in these areas. It also means developing and tapping teacher leadership to provide assistance in these areas.

. . . .

Today I will select an area of instructional leadership that I believe will make a significant difference and determine an action I will take, no matter how small, to make progress in that area.

44

Define Your Professional Purpose

Education has to be about lifting limitations on ourselves and on others.
—Paul D. Houston

Leaders who are guided and energized by their deepest purposes can better sustain their commitment to worthy goals over many months and years. These purposes may include giving all youngsters a decent chance at a successful life, preparing students for civic engagement and gainful employment, and supporting all students in understanding and more fully using their talents in ways that enhance their own lives and the lives of others. Closely linked to these broader purposes is the intention of having all students experience high-quality learning every day and be surrounded by supportive relationships.

* *

Today I will draft a brief statement of my professional purpose. I will make a note to return to it again in the near future to continue to refine its clarity and precision.

45

Be a Teacher

Teaching is the most effective means by which a leader can lead.
—Noel M. Tichy

Effective leaders are teachers. Their "classroom" is the school community, their "students" are the members of that community, and they "teach" their "lessons" in many formal and informal ways. The purpose of leaders' teaching is to stimulate new habits of mind and behavior that unleash the community's potential to realize its most important aspirations. While such teaching can take many forms, it addresses both heads and hearts and is guided by a deep respect for and responsiveness to the inner lives and professional judgment of community members.

• • • • • • • • • • • • • • • • • • • •

Today I will determine a subject about which I would like to cultivate a deeper understanding in the school community (for instance, professional community) and identify a means by which I will develop that understanding, such as dialogue in a committee meeting or discussion of an article in a faculty meeting.

46

Cultivate Professional Judgment

> We have to change and reform the education system so that we're cap-
> turing both the left and the right sides of the kid's brain. . . . Otherwise,
> we end up with an education system that's like a data download—a
> great database but no processor.
>
> *—Mike Huckabee*

One of leaders' most important responsibilities is the cultivation of professional judgment throughout the school community, beginning with themselves. The cultivation of professional judgment requires time and space for
meaningfully processing the "data download" of experiences, professional
literature, and professional development that can overwhelm the brain's
ability to make sense of it. Such processing requires intellectually rigorous
activities such as writing, discussing, and deeply examining important issues that fully engage teachers' and principals' brains in robust ways that
create new neural networks or enrich existing ones.

. . . .

Today I will nurture my professional judgment by developing a more
nuanced view of a subject of importance to the school community. I will
express my view in writing to better assess its clarity.

47

Nurture Trust

The research suggests that walkthroughs can play a constructive role only when districts make their purpose clear and carry them out in a climate of trust.

—*Jane L. David*

Leaders' cultivation of trust within in the school community is essential to the continuous improvement of teaching and learning and the strengthening of relationships. The success of structural changes (for instance, creating the position of instructional coaches) and the application of technical skills (conducting productive walkthroughs) ultimately depends on the quality of relationships among the adults in schools. Therefore, leaders must exemplify trustworthiness in all their relationships, particularly their consistency in doing what they say they will do and their honesty with everyone in all situations.

. . . .

Today I will courageously assess the extent to which I embody trustworthiness. I will select an aspect of trustworthiness that could be strengthened and take an action, no matter how small, to improve it.

48

Demonstrate Empathy, Caring, and Cooperation

> Take time out of the curriculum to teach students to manage their emotions and to practice empathy, caring, and cooperation—and their academic achievement could improve in the bargain.
>
> *—Debra Viadero*

Schools will succeed in nurturing students' empathy, caring, and cooperation to the extent those qualities are intentionally nurtured in teachers. Empathy, caring, and cooperation among adults are essential ingredients in productive school cultures, qualities which in turn contribute to student achievement. The development of empathy, caring, and cooperation in the school community requires that leaders begin by changing themselves so that what they believe, understand, say, and do each day is aligned with those attributes.

. . . .

Today I will be alert for situations in which I can authentically express empathy, caring, and a spirit of cooperation.

49

Match Words and Deeds

We define integrity—a key ingredient in character and a primary spiritual muscle—as doing what you say you are going to do when you say you are going to do it.

—*Jim Loehr & Tony Schwartz*

Leaders' integrity is a wellspring of their influence within the school community. A core attribute of leaders' integrity is their consistency in doing what they say they will do. When leaders encourage others to keep their promises, they promote integrity throughout the school community. Teachers' accountability to each other sustains continuous improvements in teaching and learning far more effectively than external forms of accountability to state or federal entities. Such peer-to-peer influence is the bedrock of interpersonal accountability.

. . . .

Today I will reflect on the congruence between my words and deeds and reaffirm my desire to keep all my promises, both large and small.

50

Speak Your Vision

Speaking a vision transforms the speaker.

—*Rosamund Stone Zander & Benjamin Zander*

The words leaders speak—particularly when their words express their deepest aspirations and values—change leaders themselves as well as influence others. When leaders describe the qualities of the school community they want to cocreate with others, they gain personal clarity and promote learning in others. Also, when members of the school community gain clarity about and express their collective aspirations, their words become a source of energy and courage that sustains the challenging work of school transformation.

. . . .

Today I will describe to someone my vision for the school community using as many specific, concrete details as possible to promote my own learning and that of others.

5I

Pay Attention to What You Learn on the Way to Your Goal

All the best ideas come out of the process; they come out of the work itself. Things occur to you. . . . It's really, really important to keep continuity and keep momentum going.

—*Chuck Close*

Important but often unpredictable insights are often the byproduct of engaging in significant work. "Doing" the work of instructional and school improvement, and reflecting on the consequences of individual and collective actions, almost always leads to significant learning that will have future applications. Progress can be guided and motivated by both the plans that initiate and set the direction of the work and the learning that occurs during the implementation process.

. . . .

Today I will reflect on the outcome of a recent action I took related to the school's long-term plan to determine what I learned that will be useful in the continuation of that work.

52

Evoke Emotion to Inspire Action and Stimulate Learning

> The French psychologist Bernard Rime has found that people almost compulsively share emotional experiences (both positive and negative), and the more intense the emotion, the more likely they are to talk about it.
>
> —*Dan Heath & Chip Heath*

Emotions can promote learning and inspire individual and collective action. Skillful leaders understand the role that emotions play in engaging people in the pursuit of shared purposes, in sustaining improvement efforts, and in stimulating learning. They tap emotion through storytelling and the use of images, metaphors, and poetry, among other means, to remind the school of its history and values and to focus the school community on a common vision.

. . . .

Today I will look for an opportunity to use a story or other means of evoking emotion to motivate or guide action and to stimulate learning.

53

Use Your Capacities

> If you deliberately plan to be less than you are capable of becoming,
> then I warn you that you'll be deeply unhappy for the rest of your life.
> You will be evading your capacities, your own possibilities.
>
> —*Abraham Maslow*

Human capacities clamor to be used and, when untapped, can be a source of chronic frustration and low morale. Effective leaders value and consistently use their talents and encourage others in the school community to do the same. When leaders squander their talents and do not recognize the strengths within the school community, the community loses important resources, and the resulting unhappiness infects the school culture.

. . . .

Today I will assess how frequently I use my top three strengths. I will determine a way that at least one of them could be applied today.

54

Invent Your Way Into the Future

In the realm of possibility, we gain our knowledge by invention.
—Rosamund Stone Zander & Benjamin Zander

The invention of solutions within a unique school context (rather than rep-lication of others' "best practices") is an important and underused means of solving classroom and school problems. Invention is founded on the belief that a preferred future can be created, even when the pathway ahead is not clear. It is also founded on the assumption that the process of invention can generate useful practices and knowledge that cannot be found elsewhere.

. . . .

Today I will invent a solution to a problem. I will describe the solution to one or more people to test its viability before implementing it.

55

Be Present

Be here. Be present. Wherever you are, be there.

—*Willie Nelson*

Present-moment awareness is an important means to improve communication, strengthen relationships, and promote learning. Leaders' relationships are deepened, as is professional learning, when leaders are fully present and open to what they are experiencing. Because many forces impede present-moment awareness, its cultivation requires intention and diligent practice.

. . . .

Today I will strive to be fully present, if even for just a few minutes, in at least one situation. If I find my mind drifting, I will patiently return it to the present moment.

56

Be Efficacious

There is much research to confirm the importance of a sense of efficacy—
the sense of making a meaningful difference, of true accomplishment—in
teachers' motivation and performance.

—*Robert Evans*

Leaders who believe their daily actions make a difference increase their own
motivation and the motivation of others and are more likely to achieve the
results they most desire. Leaders who feel helpless and hopeless about the
future unwittingly create similar feelings in others. Like teachers, leaders
who believe that their efforts matter can better sustain the demanding work
of changing their beliefs, understandings, and actions to benefit all students.

· · · · · · · · · · · · · · · · · · · ·

Today I will conduct an honest self-assessment of my sense of efficacy
and how it affects others, positively or negatively. To promote a feeling of
efficacy, I will make note of situations in which I made a positive difference.

57

Attend to the Soul

To teach in a manner that respects and cares for the souls of our students is essential if we are to provide the necessary conditions where learning can most deeply and ultimately begin.

—bell hooks

Leaders who respect and care for the humanity of all adults and young people in their charge are far more likely to lead schools where inspiring teaching and learning occurs in every classroom. These leaders begin by listening to and caring for the deep and enduring aspects of their own humanity. Because members of the school community bring their entire being—intellect, body, emotions, and spirit—into the schoolhouse, leaders who attend to the whole person unleash individual and collective potential.

. . . .

Today I will spend a few minutes in silence to invite into my awareness the "small, still voice" that is often unheard within the din of busy professional lives. I will note what it tells me.

58

Question Your Assumptions

Don't believe everything you think.

—Bumper sticker

The achievement of important goals requires that leaders periodically examine their most important assumptions and ideas to determine their current relevance. Beliefs and ideas can outlive their usefulness if they are not reviewed and updated based on new experiences and learning. Such an examination is best undertaken within a trusting community in which leaders carefully consider the perspectives of others to determine which assumptions and ideas are due to be refined or replaced.

. . . .

Today I will identify an important but perhaps outmoded professional assumption and discuss it with one or more respected colleagues to determine its current relevance. I will be open to their influence and will reformulate my assumption, if appropriate.

59

Notice and Tell Stories

Leaders must tell stories of who they are and the values they hold. They must tell stories of where the organization is at that moment in time, and they must build a shared vision for where they are headed.

—*Sam Intrator & Megan Scribner*

Leaders extend their influence when they tell stories that explain core values and illustrate the school community's vision. Human beings are hardwired to attend to stories; as a result, stories are an effective means of influence because they can touch the heart as well as the mind. School leaders are fortunate to be surrounded by stories that just await their notice, stories that vividly illustrate important cultural or instructional attributes from the perspective of students, teachers, parents, and other community members.

. . . .

Today I will be watchful for anecdotes I can share with others to illustrate important values, ideas, or practices.

60

Be Positive

> The single most important factor in predicting organizational performance . . . was the ratio of positive statements to negative statements. Positive statements are those that express appreciation, support, helpfulness, approval, or compliments. Negative statements express criticism, disapproval, dissatisfaction, cynicism, or disparagement. . . . Five times more positive statements were made than negative statements as high-performing teams engaged in work.
>
> —*Kim Cameron*

Leaders' positivity affects an organization's overall emotional tone. When the ratio of leaders' positive-to-negative statements is high, the school community becomes more appreciative and respectful. Increasing the number of positive statements increases positive emotions, which in turn provides a steady flow of positive energy essential to continuous improvement.

. . . .

Today I will keep a careful tally of the number of positive and negative comments I make to determine their relative proportions. If necessary, I will set a goal to increase the number of positive comments in future interactions.

61

Attend Deeply to Others

> People yearn to be heard. From teenagers, to middle-level managers, to the infirm in hospital beds, to politicians on the floor of the statehouse, there is a yearning to be taken seriously, to be respected, to be attended to by another.
>
> —*Sam Intrator & Megan Scribner*

Attentive, mindful listening transforms relationships and promotes learning on the part of both speaker and listener. Leaders who demonstrate deep respect for and openness to being influenced through their committed listening give a gift to both themselves and to those with whom they interact. Such listening has as its only goal truly understanding the perspective and meaning offered by the speaker.

. . . .

Today I will listen deeply to one or more people without interruption, judgment, or contradiction. I will thank them for honestly sharing their views with me, particularly if those views vary from my own.

62

Identify Multiple Solutions to Problems

Most of us are brought up to find *the* right answer rather than an answer to questions. We do not easily come up with several alternatives.

—*Ellen Langer*

Most problems of teaching and learning can be addressed in a number of ways. "One-right-way" thinking dictates a single solution and narrows the range of approaches from which leaders and members of the school community may choose when addressing school improvement challenges. It also can lead to prematurely settling on the first solution the individual or group identifies, although that solution is less than optimal. One-right-way thinking can also lead to dependence on experts rather than tap into and develop the community's problem-solving capacity.

. . . .

Today I will brainstorm at least five potential solutions to a problem and carefully consider each option before determining a course of action, recognizing that each option may contain a part of the solution. If helpful, I will invite others in the school community to brainstorm solutions with me.

63

Strengthen Cultural Support for Professional Learning

Principals play the key role in creating a context of culture in which adult learning flourishes.

—*Pam Robbins & Harvey Alvy*

Effective school leaders understand that school culture and organizational context have a profound effect on professional learning and the implementation of new practices. Adult learning is stimulated or inhibited by the cultures in which it occurs. New practices are tested and refined in cultures that are collaborative and trusting and that encourage experimentation and risk taking.

* * * * * * * * * * * * * * * * * * *

Today I will candidly assess my organization's culture in terms of its support for collaboration, experimentation, and continuous improvement, and determine a next step in an area I would like to strengthen.

64

Live an Examined Life

> As leaders, we all have an obligation to engage in self-reflection lest we lead unconsciously or mindlessly. . . . Socrates said that the unexamined life is not worth living. Now that I am old enough to amend Socrates instead of merely quoting him, I want to add one thing, for the record: if you decide to live an unexamined life, please do not take a job that involves other people.
>
> —*Parker Palmer*

Creating schools in which both young people and adults thrive requires that leaders reflect on their most important purposes and methods. Leaders who think deeply about what they are doing, why they are doing it, and the effects their actions have on others not only improve their effectiveness, but also model for the school community the value of such reflection. Leaders and the organizations they lead also benefit when leaders' reflections include the broader purposes, values, and activities of their lives.

* *

Today I will take a few minutes to examine in writing the alignment between my most important values and goals and a recent action of some significance. I will also consider the extent to which the results matched my intentions.

65

Create Space

> What makes a fire burn
> is space between the logs,
> a breathing space.
>
> *—Judy Brown*

Leaders who create "white space" in their calendars to reflect on and derive meaning from their experiences are more effective in creating the results they most desire. Even a few minutes of "think time" between meetings can provide an opportunity to calm the mind, reflect on the last event, and prepare for the next activity. Also, "micro-think time" found in the space between the speaking of one person and the response of another offers an opportunity for reflection on what was said, what it means, and what the speaker or the listener might say next.

. . . .

Today I will create a few minutes of white space in my calendar or slow down the pace of a conversation to gain a sense of perspective and to synthesize what I have experienced.

66

Master Yourself

> Knowing others is intelligence; knowing yourself is true wisdom. Mastering others is strength; mastering yourself is true power.
>
> —*Tao Te Ching #33*

Leaders who possess the knowledge and skills associated with emotional self-mastery are far more likely to create and sustain cultures of mutual respect and trust. Such skills enable leaders to identify their own feelings, express them constructively, and consider the effects on others of their communication and actions. The cultivation of these skills also enables leaders to understand and honor the perspectives and feelings of others, which is an important step in achieving communitywide consensus on important issues and in determining win-win solutions to problems.

. . . .

Today I will reflect on my awareness of my own and others' feelings, my empathy regarding the experiences and perspectives of others, and the respectfulness of my communication.

67

Experience Genuine Teamwork

> The kinds of errors that cause plane crashes are invariably errors of teamwork and communication. One pilot knows something important and somehow doesn't tell the other pilot. One pilot does something wrong, and the other pilot doesn't catch the error.
>
> —*Malcolm Gladwell*

Creating schools that produce high levels of learning for all students requires genuine teamwork at all levels. That means that teamwork among leaders is a prerequisite to the establishment of teamwork among teachers. When leaders experience teamwork with their colleagues, they better understand and are more skillful at addressing the issues that arise in establishing and sustaining teamwork in their schools. Such teamwork among leaders requires meaningful, stretching goals that cannot be accomplished unless leaders truly collaborate.

. . . .

Today I will consider whether I am a member of a truly interdependent leadership team. If I determine that leaders are essentially a group of independent contractors rather than a fully functioning team, I will raise this issue with my colleagues.

68

Speak Concisely

He can compress the most words into the smallest idea of any man I know.
—Abraham Lincoln

A hallmark of leaders' influence is their ability to speak and write concisely and with precision. Leaders' clarity is essential to their effectiveness and is closely linked to their ability to speak and write clearly and succinctly. Because complex and abstract language is sometimes mistakenly viewed as a sign of intelligence, leaders may underestimate the importance of their clarity on the school community's understanding of its collective vision, values, purposes, and methods.

Today I will take a few moments to prepare myself to speak clearly during an upcoming conversation or meeting. I will do my best to get to the point quickly, stop when I have made that point, and listen carefully to the views of others.

69

Stand for Profound Purposes

> If a school does not stand for something more profound than raising
> achievement levels, then it probably does not make a memorable dif-
> ference to teachers, students, and parents.
>
> —*Terrence E. Deal & Kent D. Peterson*

Effective leaders cocreate with their school communities a vision that
transcends test scores and other limited measures of student success. While
test scores may be viewed by some politicians and the general public as the
primary measure of educational quality, wise leaders know they are only
one indicator of success. Consequently, such leaders engage the school
community in sustained dialogue regarding purposes and values that goes
above and beyond the knowledge and skills typically measured by stan-
dardized achievement tests.

. . . .

Today I will consider whether my school's vision and the conversations
that occur in faculty meetings reflect purposes that transcend test scores
and issues of school management. If such topics are largely absent, I will
take a few minutes to clarify what I think is missing and determine a time
when I can converse with the school community about it.

70

Open Minds by Touching Hearts

Minds are very hard things to open, and the best way to open the mind is through the heart.

—*Jonathan Haidt*

Leaders extend their influence when they speak to the heart as well as the head. Human beings are motivated at least as much by their emotions as they are by logic and rationality. While research, data, and other forms of evidence have their place in improvement efforts, by themselves they are insufficient. Emotions elicited through storytelling, poetry, and the use of imagery can inspire and provide a context for the meaningful use of data and professional literature.

* * * * * * * * * * * * * * * * * * *

Today I will speak to the heart as well as the head in an upcoming interaction with colleagues, students, or parents.

71

Adapt

Great districts constantly learn from one another, but they never make the mistake of trying to cut and paste success from one context to another.
—*Megan Tupa & Ledyard McFadden*

Continuous improvement in schools is essentially a process of inventions, improvisation, and adaptation. It builds on the discoveries and findings of others rather than seeks to replicate their procedures and practices in a lock-step fashion. Because organizational context and culture affect implementation of new practices, "best" practices cannot be imported into a school or classroom without some modification.

. . . .

Today I will identify a way to use the work of researchers or the best practices of other schools to stimulate invention and professional learning and to inform professional judgment in ways that will lead to the appropriate implementation of new practices and to improved results.

72

Communicate Respect to Extend Influence

The best way to win over opponents is to accept that they have legitimate concerns, for that triggers an instinct to reciprocate.

—*Nicholas Kristof*

Leaders who communicate genuine respect for the views of others are more influential than those who do not. Respecting others' views does not necessarily mean agreeing with them, but rather regarding their perspectives as worthy of a fair hearing. And when school community members feel that their perspectives are respected, they are far more likely to be receptive to and influenced by their leaders' views.

. . . .

Today I will invite someone to share his or her perspective with me, give it careful consideration, and demonstrate that I have heard and valued it before stating my viewpoint.

73

Learn and Teach

Leaders build time into their calendars for teaching and reflection.

—*Noel M. Tichy*

Effective leaders are both learners and teachers. They make their own professional learning a priority, a good portion of which occurs through methods that are close at hand—daily periods of reflection, journal reading, data analysis, and conversations with colleagues. These leaders continuously look for opportunities to teach others about their most important values, purposes, and ideas. Such teaching, however, is seldom offered in a "stand-and-deliver" format; it is far more likely to be conversation-based and "just in time" as it informs pressing issues of professional practice.

. . . .

Today I will identify an upcoming opportunity to teach others about values or ideas that are important to the school community.

74

Use the Gap

Leaders live in the gap between what should be and what is. That is where the work that most needs doing resides.

—*Sam Intrator & Megan Scribner*

The school community's focus and momentum is maintained when leaders successfully manage the tension that resides in the gap between current reality and the school's stretching vision of a preferred future. Effective leaders do not succumb to pressure to deny or minimize current reality or to reduce the reach of the vision of a desired future. The tension inherent in this gap spurs action that expands the school community's capacity to create the new reality embodied in the vision. Without the gap, there is little tension, and without the tension, there is little action.

Today I will briefly describe in my own words my view of current reality and the school community's vision for its preferred future to determine the stretch contained in the gap. I will identify the next step I or we will take to close the gap.

75

Write to Clarify Thinking

Clear thinking becomes clear writing: one can't exist without the other.
—*William Zinsser*

Writing is a powerful and underused tool that enables leaders to clarify their thinking and communicate effectively with the school community. Writing can serve many purposes. Leaders can write to clarify the purpose of an upcoming meeting or conversation, to explain a value or principle they are applying in making a critical decision, or to express the essence of an idea that is important to the school community.

. . . .

Today I will use the process of writing to clarify a subject of importance to me. I will review my writing later in the day and make notes on any new insights that may have arisen.

76

Consider Your Impact

> With every act of leadership, large and small, we help cocreate the reality in which we live, from the microcosm of personal relationships to the macrocosm of war and peace. . . . I am responsible for my impact on the world whether I acknowledge it or not.
>
> —*Parker Palmer*

Leaders' thoughts, words, and actions significantly influence others and, through them, profoundly affect the future. Leaders begin by recognizing and assuming responsibility for their influence, in whatever ways that influence manifests itself. They then consider the effects they *intend to have* and periodically reflect on the impact they *are having* on those around them.

· · · · · · · · · · · · · · · · · · · ·

Today I will complete the following sentence: "The effects I want my thoughts, words, and actions to have on others are . . ." I will choose the words I speak and the actions I take with an awareness of my responsibility for the consequences of my actions.

77

See Through the Eyes of Others

Empathy is the ability to imagine yourself in someone else's position and to intuit what that person is feeling. It is the ability to stand in others' shoes, to see with their eyes, and to feel with their hearts. . . . But empathy isn't sympathy—that is, feeling bad for someone else. It is feeling with someone else, sensing what it would be like to be that person.

—Daniel Pink

A leader's ability to see the world through the eyes of others is an essential tool in forming satisfying and productive relationships and in shaping organizational culture. Understanding and valuing others' reality, especially when it is not the leader's own reality, demonstrates respect and deepens trust. It also embodies the fundamental leadership practice, "Seek first to understand."

. . . .

Today I will demonstrate that I have heard someone else's perspective by expressing it in a way that causes the person to believe that I really "get it."

78

Use Visual Language

Vision is visual. There are many benefits to a visual language. One is the amount of information that a picture contains. . . . You can see the relationships among the various parts. Also, thinking in pictures forces you to be concrete. There is little room for the vague, because you will not be able to see a picture unless you have decided on vital elements of the creation.

—Robert Fritz

Leaders' use of a richly detailed visual language to describe an intended future focuses and guides the school community. When leaders use concrete, descriptive words and phrases, they support the development of a common understanding of abstract ideas that enables wise decision-making and incremental progress toward the new reality. Image-evoking vision statements create in the collective mind's eye of the school community a vivid, magnet-like representation of a preferred future that draws the school community toward it.

. . . .

Today I will consider the extent to which the school's vision or mission statement employs a visual language that turns vague and abstract ideas into images that school community members can literally see in their minds' eyes.

79

Slow Down

> Speed itself has snuck up on us. It has gradually become a way of life we are now addicted to and complacent with without even knowing it. . . . To maintain our sanity in such an era, we may have to become intimate with stillness, every one of us. . . . I am not talking about leisure time. I am talking about non-doing.
>
> —*Jon Kabat-Zinn*

Leaders' ability to periodically slow down their minds and bodies enhances their emotional well-being and aids their intellectual clarity. Leaders' calmness and clarity are essential leadership tools that profoundly affect the school community. Both qualities are enhanced when leaders slow themselves down, even if only for a few minutes at a time.

. . . .

Today I will take five minutes to do nothing. I will close my office door and resist the lure of email notifications and text messages. I will arrive a few minutes early for a meeting, sitting quietly in my car or the meeting room awaiting the arrival of others.

80

Stimulate Complex, Intelligent Behavior

Have a simple, clear purpose which gives rise to complex, intelligent behavior, rather than complex rules and regulations that give rise to simplistic thinking and stupid behavior.

—Dee Hock

Leaders who express their purposes in clear, succinct ways and who stimulate the cultivation and use of professional judgment in others extend their influence throughout the school community. Conversely, leaders' use of bureaucratic rules and regulations to mandate certain behaviors produces resistance and, at best, low-level compliance. Leaders' clear expression and the use of that clarity to cultivate professional judgment throughout the organization is a "force multiplier" that improves the quality of thought and action at all levels, from the classroom through administrative offices.

* * * * * * * * * * * * * * * * * * * *

Today I will refine and polish an important purpose or idea until I get to its core and interact with others to cultivate their judgment regarding how and when it would be best implemented in this setting.

81

Plant a Tree

The best time to plant a tree is twenty years ago.
The next best time is today.

—*African proverb*

Leaders who provide a hopeful orientation about the future generate positive energy and help their organizations maintain a solution-oriented approach to current challenges. These leaders continuously seek ways to advance the mission of their schools rather than nurture regrets or dwell on past mistakes. They engage others in problem solving rather than in assignment of blame.

· · · · · · · · · · · · · · · · · · · ·

Today I will conduct an honest self-assessment of my hopefulness about the future and ability to focus on solutions rather than past mistakes.

82

Align Actions With Vision

A task without a vision is drudgery. A vision without a task is but a dream. But a vision with a task is the hope of the world.

—Anonymous

Effective leaders combine a compelling purpose with a steady stream of goal-focused actions to produce continuous improvements in teaching, learning, and relationships. They understand that a purpose without meaningful actions on its behalf is merely a fervent wish. On the other hand, actions taken without a compelling purpose are unfocused and seldom create or sustain commitment to the demanding work of continuous improvement.

. . . .

Today I will examine the alignment of the school community's actions with its vision. I will have conversations with others in the school community about ways that alignment can be improved.

83

Strengthen Relationships With Those Closest to You

> Almost every problem of the community, state, and nation is met with on a small scale in our relations with people closest to us. Unless we can be successful in those relationships, we have not yet mastered the art of building a community. We need not wait for great programs. Each person in his day-to-day relationships can be mastering the art of community.
>
> —*Arthur E. Morgan*

A starting point in the creation of meaningful professional communities is leaders attending to the quality of relationships closest to them. Cultural change begins in those interactions and spreads slowly throughout the organization. In all their relationships, leaders can cultivate mutual respect, trust, caring, clarity of purpose, and mutual accountability. As community members experience these qualities in their relationships with leaders, they in turn begin to interact in new and more positive ways with their colleagues.

. . . .

Today I will select a relationship that is particularly important to me and assess its quality in terms of mutual respect, trust, caring, clarity of purpose, and accountability. If appropriate, I will identify an action I will soon take to strengthen that relationship.

84

Open Yourself to the Views of Others

Courage is what it takes to stand up and speak. Courage is also what it takes to sit down and listen.

—Winston Churchill

Leaders who practice the discipline of committed listening and demonstrate openness to the views of others increase their influence in their school communities. Such openness, however, is a courageous act, because it may mean that leaders will learn something that will lead them to surrender a belief or an idea that no longer rings true. For many people, giving up a cherished belief or idea, even when it no longer serves them, is a very difficult thing to do.

· ·

Today I will listen carefully with a spirit of openness to someone whose views may challenge my own thinking and give thoughtful consideration to that perspective and the experiences or ideas that shaped it.

85

Acquire New Habits of Mind and Practice

Even while we're creating new "neural pathways," the old ones are still there in our brains. Until the new ones become completely second nature, then stress or fear can make us fall back on the old ones.

—*Alan Deutschman*

The practice of school leadership is governed to a large degree by habits of mind and behavior. When those habits no longer serve an organization's purposes, successful leaders develop new habits that support the achievement of important goals. These leaders create or strengthen already-existing neural networks that manifest themselves in new ways of thinking, speaking, and acting. Given the tenacity of old habits, they understand that creating new ones is a demanding task that requires intention, attention, and persistence across many weeks or months until mastery is achieved.

· · · · · · · · · · · · · · · · · · · ·

Today I will identify a habit that I want to cultivate in support of an important school goal and take the first step in practicing a new way of thinking or behaving. I will seek the encouragement and support of a colleague in establishing the habit.

86

Collect Stories

Stories capture the context, capture the emotions. . . . [T]hey encapsulate, into one compact package, information, knowledge, context, and emotion.
—*Donald Norman*

Skillful leaders use stories to help others understand ideas and to motivate improvement efforts. They know that stories give meaning to abstract concepts and help members of the school community see how new ideas and practices are connected to larger purposes and to one another. These leaders also understand that stories speak to the heart in ways that research, data, and professional literature seldom do.

• • • • • • • • • • • • • • • • • • • •

Today I will explore the mental archives of my experience to retrieve a story that illustrates an important attribute of a significant school goal and will look for opportunities to share it with others.

87

Speak Forthrightly

Leadership is found most often in simple acts of self-expression, when conscience overcomes reticence and we make our presence known by challenging a falsehood that has been advertised as truth, calling injustice by its name, stopping to help another, or on one memorable occasion, daring to take a seat at the front of the bus.

—*Madeleine K. Albright*

Speaking with candor is a hallmark of a leader's integrity. Candor is supported by two primary attributes: clarity and courage. Leaders cannot speak or act forthrightly if they cannot express in simple terms the values or principles that affect their actions. Because expressing one's truth in some settings may have negative consequences, it can be a courageous act. Consequently, such candor is founded on a clear understanding of one's most important values and purposes.

· · · · · · · · · · · · · · · · · · · ·

Today I will identify an occasion when candid speaking will best serve the school community's values and purposes, and I will clarify what I might say in that situation.

88

Cultivate Gratitude

> Gratitude has been found to have dramatic effects on individual and group performance.... Emmons also found that expressions of gratitude by one person tended to motivate others to express gratitude, so a self-perpetuating, virtuous cycle occurred when gratitude was expressed.
>
> —*Kim Cameron*

Leaders who express genuine gratitude help create positive emotions in their school communities. Leaders begin by increasing their awareness of daily events, large and small, for which they are thankful. They then appropriately communicate that gratitude in conversations, meetings, and other venues.

. . . .

Today I will note in writing several things for which I am grateful and communicate them to others when appropriate. I will consider extending that practice for a week or more and pay attention to its effects on my mood and relationships.

89

Act Intentionally to Change Culture

Probably the most important—and the most difficult—job of the school-based reformer is to change the prevailing culture . . . Ultimately, a school's culture has far more influence on life and learning in the schoolhouse than the state department of education, the superintendent, the school board, or even the principal can ever have.

—*Roland S. Barth*

One important responsibility of leaders is to shape school cultures that enable continuous improvement. Not all cultures are created equal in their ability to nurture and sustain new professional understandings and practices. That means that leaders intentionally nurture cultures with high levels of respect, trust, caring, and interpersonal accountability. Creating and sustaining such cultures requires persistence in the face of the many challenges that will arise.

· ·

Today I will select an important element of school culture—perhaps one of those suggested in this publication—and identify an action I will take on its behalf.

90

Use Problems to Promote Learning

We put problems on students' plates that don't already have a solution.

—*Alex Alvarez*

Skillful leaders view problems as valuable learning opportunities for both students and adults alike. Problem-based inquiry provides both a context and a reason for learning, whether the learner is a five-year-old beginning school or a fifty-five-year-old seeking ways to improve his or her professional practice. Grappling with real-life problems—those without predetermined right answers—stimulates and guides continuous improvement efforts.

. . . .

Today I will select a problem as a source of important learning for the school community and consider ways I can productively engage others with it to stimulate reflection, learning, and action.

91

Use Conversations to Spread Influence

> While no single conversation is guaranteed to change the trajectory of a career, a relationship, or a life, any single conversation can.
>
> —*Susan Scott*

Leaders who view every conversation as a possible means for professional learning and improvement dramatically increase their influence within their school communities. While such conversation may occur in formal settings, such as meetings or professional learning sessions, they are often most powerful when they emerge spontaneously in response to everyday professional challenges and occur in classrooms, hallways, or offices. A candid, respectful exchange of perspectives and assumptions, combined with careful listening, can deepen understanding and affect practice.

· · · · · · · · · · · · · · · · · · · ·

Today I will act as though each conversation, no matter how brief, can stimulate important professional learning and change practice.

92

Learn and Invent in Order to Address Adaptive Challenges

Technical problems (even though they may be complex) can be solved with knowledge and procedures already in hand. In contrast, *adaptive challenges* require new learning, innovation, and new patterns of behavior.

—*Sharon Daloz Parks*

Leaders' learning and innovation within the school community are at the heart of continuous improvement in teaching and student achievement. Because many of the problems faced by school leaders are context-specific, their solutions require more than the implementation of lock-step solutions invented elsewhere. While it is important that educators' professional judgment be informed by others' experiences, successful school leaders understand that meaningful solutions must be constructed using the unique talents and resources of their own school communities.

. . . .

Today I will identify a time when this school community successfully invented a solution to a problem and reflect on what was learned from that process that could be applied to a current problem.

93

Mobilize Through Hopefulness

Leadership is about . . . mobilizing people to make progress on the hardest of problems.

—*Ron Heifetz*

Leadership for continuous improvement involves creating a sense of hopefulness that important problems can be solved and that worthy goals can be achieved. That means that leaders themselves must be hopeful and see possibility where others may only see barriers. Leaders' hopefulness is contagious and inspires the school community as it takes on the challenging tasks of establishing stretching goals, in working together in new ways, and in assessing the results of its efforts as a means of continuously improving practice.

• • • • • • • • • • • • • • • • • • • •

Today I will candidly assess my hopefulness about the possibility of a better future for the school community and consider ways my hopefulness might be strengthened and communicated to others.

94

See Underlying Relationships, Not Events

Systems thinking is a discipline for seeing wholes. It is a framework for seeing interrelationships rather than things, for seeing patterns of change rather than static snapshots.

—Peter Senge

High-functioning school communities see beyond symptoms and surface problems to underlying conditions and relationships that often profoundly influence events. They see patterns and connections among seemingly isolated incidents that are often invisible to others. To that end, leaders help schools rise above the details of their daily responsibilities to look both broadly and deeply at structures and connections among parts of the organization to determine whether they support or inhibit attainment of important goals. They do so by inviting others in the school community to explore underlying patterns with them and to reflect deeply on what they observe.

. . . .

Today I will identify several troublesome events or problems and look for underlying connections among them, keeping in mind that the links may not be immediately evident. To deepen my analysis, I will discuss my observations with others.

95

Honor Feelings

People do not resist change, per se. They resist loss.

—*Ron Heifetz & Marty Linsky*

Significant change in the professional or personal lives of educators often evokes strong emotional responses. Skillful leaders acknowledge and address the feelings of loss, anxiety, and anger that naturally arise as part of the change process by listening carefully and by honoring and respecting the perspectives of those with whom they interact. These leaders also understand that while such feelings are predictable, they cannot be allowed to take precedence over the interests of students or the continuous improvement of teaching and learning in all classrooms.

• • • • • • • • • • • • • • • • • • • •

Today I will listen carefully to the feelings of those who are most affected by improvement efforts and demonstrate that I understand their experiences without compromising the achievement of overarching purposes and goals.

96

Learn

The way to have an interesting life is to stay on the steep part of the learning curve.

—*Nolan Bushnell*

The most successful leaders in promoting learning in their schools are voracious learners themselves. These leaders set challenging goals for themselves and align their professional learning with those goals. They also are transparent in their learning and openly discuss with the school community the challenges of such learning, their successes and failures, and the effects of the learning on their day-to-day practice.

. . . .

Today I will tell a valued colleague about an important learning goal and the means by which I intend to achieve it. I will indicate on my calendar when I will update them on my progress and the effects the learning is having on my work.

97

Use Disequilibrium to Stimulate Growth

[T]he system will always seek to maintain the current equilibrium (even though it may be highly dysfunctional) rather than undergo the distress of the disequilibrium needed to move to a more adequate equilibrium.

—*Sharon Daloz Parks*

Leaders who succeed in moving their organizations to significantly higher levels of performance capitalize on the disequilibrium that accompanies change. In fact, these leaders often perturb the system to "unfreeze" old habits of mind and behavior so that new levels of performance can be achieved. At the same time, they recognize that this in-between state often produces feelings of uncertainty and even incompetence as the old and familiar fade but are not yet fully replaced by new routines and improved performance. These leaders reassure the school community that these feelings are to be expected and will be transcended by a sense of competence as new, higher-level skills are developed.

. . . .

Today I will assess the equilibrium or disequilibrium of the school community (for instance, both feet firmly planted in old ways, a state of disequilibrium between the old and the new, or both feet rooted in the new way) and act to celebrate progress and to stimulate continuing growth.

98

Be Quiet to Listen

Silence is the lost art in a society made of noise. . . . But until we are quiet and listen, we can never, ever know what is really going on—even in ourselves.

—*Joan Chittester*

Leaders who appreciate the value of stillness and quiet and regularly experience it have access to important aspects of themselves that are often hidden in the rush of daily activities. The calmness such experiences offer creates in these leaders a sensitivity to what is occurring around them that enables wiser decision-making and stronger relationships. Because our culture values "doing" over "being," slowing down to listen to one's inner voice requires leaders to intentionally develop new routines and habits.

. . . .

Today I will take a few minutes to be still and quiet. If my mind seems full of thoughts and feelings that disrupt the experience, I will simply note whatever thoughts arise without trying to direct them.

99

Tap the Community's Deepest Purposes

> Serve others. The unfailing recipe for happiness and success is to want the good of others.
>
> —Desmond Tutu

School communities that profoundly affect the lives of students and adults are motivated and guided by deeper purposes and values. These purposes often include serving others, promoting children's well-being, or contributing to the future of a better world. Leaders support the school community in identifying and connecting with collective purposes that transcend test scores or other limited measures of success. These deeper purposes fuel improvement efforts and enable the school community to stay on track with what is most important to it.

. . . .

Today I will take a moment to express in writing the fundamental purpose of my work and will share it with the school community. I will invite community members to reflect on and share with one another the deeper purposes of their work.

100

Write to Discover What You Think

> There are a thousand thoughts lying within a man that he does not know until he takes up a pen to write.
>
> —*William Makepeace Thackeray*

Writing is a powerful tool that can assist leaders in discovering what they already know and in extending their understanding of important subjects. Writing is not only a means of communicating ideas, but also a process through which leaders gain clarity and create new understandings for themselves and their school communities. Leaders share their writing to stimulate conversation to promote deeper understanding of important values and ideas.

. . . .

Today I will take a few minutes to write about a problem or situation that I do not yet fully understand and use my newfound clarity as I interact with others.

IOI

Learn From Your Childhood

We see the world clearly when we are children, and we spend the rest of our lives trying to remember what it was we saw.

—*Garrison Keillor*

Leaders who endeavor to remember and learn from their own childhoods can better lead in the creation of schools in which all children thrive. The joy of children, their enthusiasm for learning, and their openness to new experiences, among other attributes, are important qualities for leaders to recall and bring to their own work and that of the school community. Remembering their lives as children can also help leaders reaffirm some of the deeper purposes that led them to their work as educators.

. . . .

Today I will reflect on the lessons of my childhood and the wisdom and guidance they offer in my current role.

102

Promote Professional Judgment

> The essential professional development task . . . is not to insist that teachers know and use research-based practices. Rather, it is a much more complex matter of putting teachers in a position to adapt research-based practices to their particular situations.
>
> —*Gerald G. Duffy & Kathryn Kear*

Effective leaders demonstrate a deep respect for the craft knowledge and experience of their colleagues by encouraging teachers to view research-based practices as tools to continuously refine their professional judgments rather than as scripts to be mindlessly applied in all situations. These leaders view research as a tool, not a rule. To that end they promote the rigorous examination of research-based practice, enable extended conversation about that research within the school community, and expect teachers to regularly reflect on how their practice affects the learning of all students and to be open to changing it for the benefit of students.

* * * * * * * * * * * * * * * * * * * *

Today I will consider ways educational research can be used to enhance teachers' professional judgment regarding their classroom practices.

103

Delight in Meaningful, Purpose-Driven Work

The grand essentials of happiness are: something to do, something to love, and something to hope for.

—*Allan K. Chalmers*

Educators whose work is linked to important purposes can better sustain the challenging, long-term effort of school transformation. Fortunately, educators have many opportunities each day to engage in meaningful, purpose-driven activities. When leaders experience purpose in their work, they help spread a sense of purpose and positive emotions throughout the school community.

• • • • • • • • • • • • • • • • • • • •

Today I will be aware of and savor the time spent performing tasks related to important purposes.

104

Manage "Next Actions"

How different our lives are when we really know what is deeply important to us, and keeping that picture in mind, we manage ourselves each day to be and do what really matters.

—Stephen Covey

Leaders' success in improving teaching, learning, and relationships in schools is determined by their ability to maintain a continuous stream of goal-focused tasks. When leaders do not fulfill promises they have made or loose momentum on a project because their attention is diverted, they diminish both their integrity and their ability to affect the most important results to them. Next-action thinking—the discipline of always keeping in mind and managing the next step in the achievement of a goal—generates energy and increases the school community's productivity.

* *

Today I will list next actions and dates for completion for an important goal or project.

105

Find an Idea's Core

> To strip an idea down to its core, we must be masters of exclusion. We must relentlessly prioritize. Saying something short is not the mission— sound bites are not the ideal. Proverbs are the ideal. We must create ideas that are both simple and profound.
>
> *—Chip Heath & Dan Heath*

The ability to find and express the core of an idea is an essential but often underdeveloped leadership skill. Stripping an idea to its core so that others can truly understand and remember it is an intellectually demanding task. Sometimes the challenge requires separating what is central to the idea from what is marginal. At other times, the challenge is finding concrete language and images to describe abstract ideas.

. . . .

Today I will use writing or a conversation with others to find the essence of an idea and will practice expressing it with proverb-like clarity.

106

Be Clear About What You Want

You will bring into your life whatever you have the most clarity about.
The trouble is, most people have a great deal of clarity about what it is
they don't want.

—*Susan Scott*

Leaders who are clear about they want in their personal and professional
lives—in contrast to what they do not want—are more influential and
effective. Such leaders also are more purposeful in both their work and
personal lives and achieve a better work–life balance. Organizational
energy is increased and focused when leaders express what they want in
simple, concrete language and invite others to do the same in a sustained
consensus-building process.

. . . .

Today I will pay particular attention to my complaints and the things
that frustrate me for clues about what I *do* want in my work and life. I will
use that awareness to clarify an intention, determine the next step in its
achievement, and express my plan to others in clear, compelling terms
to acquire the social support and accountability that comes from such a
conversation.

107

Speak Your Truth

I wonder how many children's lives might be saved if we educators disclosed what we know to each other.

—*Roland Barth*

Important learning and action almost always occur when leaders speak their truths. One powerful way for leaders to initiate deep learning is to candidly and respectfully say what is on their minds and in their hearts, particularly when it affects teaching, learning, and children's well-being. When they proclaim "The Truth"—when they speak and act as though only one correct viewpoint exists—they deny the validity of other perspectives and suppress dialogue and learning. Speaking "their truth" means that leaders share their values, intentions, assumptions, and requests in the spirit of dialogue and with a willingness to be influenced by the perspectives of others.

. . . .

Today I will tell my truth regarding an important subject about which I have been less than fully forthcoming, and I will express my viewpoint in the spirit of dialogue as *a* truth rather than *the* truth. I will rehearse what I am going to say to make certain it is both candid and respectful.

108

Spread Positive Emotions

Emotions are contagious, and positive emotions resonate throughout an organization and into relationships with other constituents. To get extraordinary things done in extraordinary times, leaders must inspire optimal performance—and that can only be fueled with positive emotions.

—*James Kouzes & Barry Posner*

A fundamental task of leadership is to spread positive emotions throughout the school community. Leaders' positive and negative emotions move through a school or school system like a virus passed from one person to the next. Their joy and enthusiasm are contagious. So, too, is their sense of possibility and hopefulness. Likewise, leaders can infect others with their sadness, anxiety, anger, fear, cynicism, and resignation.

• • • • • • • • • • • • • • • • • • • •

Today I will honestly assess my emotional state to determine where I stand along a continuum from hopeful, positive, peaceful, and enthusiastic to worried, angry, cynical, and pessimistic. I will cultivate positive emotions in my life that I will bring into the school community.

109

Take Care of Yourself

> Great leaders . . . focus attention on developing their intellect, understanding and managing emotions, taking care of their bodies, and attending to the deep beliefs and dreams that feed their spirits.
>
> —*Richard Boyatzis & Annie McKee*

Effective leaders cultivate positive energy in themselves as a first step in cultivating it within the school community. Leaders who are physically and emotionally depleted and spiritually bereft find it difficult, if not impossible, to address the intellectual and interpersonal challenges of their demanding work. Leaders increase their energy by developing healthy eating and exercise habits, establishing positive relationships, challenging themselves intellectually, and aligning their actions with values and purposes that extend beyond immediate self-interest.

. . . .

Today I will eat energy-rich food rather than snack on sugary treats, raise my spirits by scheduling a brief activity that is enjoyable and uplifting rather than drone through a series of activities that deplete the spirit, and bring myself fully to an important task rather than multitask.

110

Display Integrity by Aligning Actions With Values

Consistency between word and deed is how people judge someone to be honest.

—James Kouzes & Barry Posner

Leaders' integrity is an essential factor in the establishment of high levels of trust because it sets the tone for the quality of relationships within the school community. One way teachers and others assess leaders' integrity is by the congruence between leaders' expressed values and their daily actions. Leaders perceived to have high integrity spend their time on activities they believe are important, such as relationship building and instructional improvement.

* *

Today I will consistently align my actions with my values and encourage others to do the same.

Create Cultures of Interpersonal Accountability

Our promises create our lives. Our promises give life to our purposes and goals. Our promises move us into action. . . . Life works to the degree that we keep our promises.

—*Dave Ellis*

In high-performance cultures, interpersonal accountability replaces mandates and high-stakes testing as the primary motivating force in the continuous improvement of teaching and learning. In these cultures, members of the school community make and keep promises to steadily increase the learning of all their students—in particular, those students who have failed to meet agreed-on standards. Leaders lead in the creation of such cultures through their own accountability in keeping promises.

• •

Today I will assess whether I keep the promises I make in areas large and small, and I will make only promises that I know I can fulfill.

II2

Focus Attention on High-Impact Activities

Much of our present struggles with our organizations have to do with remembering what is essential and placing it back in the center of our lives.
—*David Whyte*

Effective leaders relentlessly focus on a small number of areas they believe will have the greatest impact on teaching, learning, and relationships in schools. A key to leaders' success in today's high-pressure environment is their ability to reduce time spent in areas that make little difference so that they can increase the amount of time they spend on the relatively few categories of activities that have the greatest impact on the achievement of their goals. Leaders begin by accepting responsibility for using their time in ways that will produce the results they most value.

. . . .

Today I will set aside a few minutes to determine the actions that will have the greatest impact on the achievement of important goals and those that will make little or no difference. I will carve out time for high-impact activities by eliminating or minimizing those that are less effective.

113

Cultivate the Problem-Solving Abilities of Others

> If you treat an individual as he is, he will stay as he is, but if you treat him as if he were what he ought to be and could be, he will become what he ought and could be.
>
> —*Johann Wolfgang von Goethe*

Wise leaders trust teachers to solve the vast majority of their own problems. Leaders who assume responsibility for the problems of others typically have little time or energy left over to focus on essential tasks to the achievement of their organizations' goals and that only they can perform. When leaders solve problems for others, they create dependency, cause atrophy in teachers' problem-solving abilities, and diminish important opportunities for professional learning that can occur only when teachers assume responsibility for their problems and grapple with solutions.

. . . .

Today I will act in ways consistent with the belief that teachers already possess or can acquire the skills to solve most of their own problems. To that end, I will more frequently serve as a committed listener to enable teachers to clarify their own problems and identify solutions.

114

Develop Supportive Relationships With Colleagues

> Principals are effective not because of positional power, but because of the synergy that flows from positive relationships between the principal and teacher—and among the teachers themselves.
>
> —*Joanne Rooney*

Leaders of schools that continuously improve the learning of all students surround teachers with relationships that offer hope and provide support in the acquisition of new practices and ways of thinking about teaching and learning. A starting place in forming such a culture among teachers is for leaders to develop relationships with one another that embody the culture they seek to create among teachers. As a result, leaders will be team members rather than work in isolation, and their relationships will exhibit high levels of trust and appreciation rather than distrust, withholding, and negativity.

· · · · · · · · · · · · · · · · · · · ·

Today I will strengthen a relationship with a colleague to inspire hope, to provide mutual support in problem solving and the development of new habits, and to stimulate new ways of thinking.

II5

Reframe Ideas to Serve School Goals

> One of the fundamental findings of cognitive science is that people think in terms of frames and metaphors. . . . The frames are in the synapses of our brains, physically present in the form of neural circuitry. When the facts don't fit the frames, the frames are kept and facts ignored. . . . Frames once entrenched are hard to dispel.
>
> —*George Lakoff*

Leaders' actions are profoundly influenced by *conceptual frames*, which are deeply rooted, beneath-the-surface systems of beliefs and ideas that affect how leaders think about teaching, learning, and leadership. A starting point in "reframing" is to articulate the current frame (for instance, students from low-income families cannot be expected to learn at high levels) and to conceptualize alternative frames that better serve student learning (for instance, the level of student learning is primarily determined by the quality of teaching and relationships in this school community). This reciprocal process engages leaders and others in the school community in mutual learning.

* *

Today I will think deeply about an important conceptual frame I currently possess about teaching and learning and consider whether reframing may be desirable in the achievement of a school goal. I will sketch out my new frame in writing.

116

Set Micro-Goals to Establish Momentum

Seek the small improvement one day at a time. That's the only way it happens—and when it happens, it lasts.

—*John Wooden*

School communities that make continuous progress in teaching and learning understand the power of small, carefully selected actions that, over time, produce substantial improvements. A micro-goal is an action at which failure in its accomplishment is unlikely but whose cumulative effect over many weeks and months can be profound. When these small goals are closely linked to the school community's most important purposes, their achievement sustains long-term focus and energy.

* *

Today I will select an area of improvement in which a micro-goal would help me establish momentum and take an action for which success is likely.

117

Respect Human Dignity

Injuries to individual and collective dignity may represent a hitherto un-recognized pathogenic force with a destructive capacity toward physical, mental, and social well-being at least equal to that of viruses or bacteria.

—*Jonathan Mann*

Respect for human dignity is essential to the formation and maintenance of caring, trusting school communities. Lack of respect can be a toxic force that destroys relationships and undermines a school's ability to achieve its most important purposes. When leaders consistently offer respect in their words and deeds, it spreads like a positive contagion to teachers, parents, and students.

· ·

Today I will reflect on specific and concrete ways that I can manifest respect for human dignity in word and deed and determine opportunities available today to demonstrate my respect for others.

118

Evoke Feelings

That which is spoken from the heart is heard by the heart.

—Jewish saying

Emotions often trump facts; a change in feelings often precedes a change in thinking and the successful implementation of new practices. While discussions of data, research, and professional literature are important in supporting the value of new practices, leaders who speak from their hearts to the hearts of those they lead help create and maintain a steady flow of energy across many months and years.

• •

Today I will touch the hearts of others when I speak authentically from my heart about events that shaped and led me into teaching and school leadership.

119

Tell Stories That Motivate and Guide

Good storytellers heal the world.... They open us up to new understanding and growth.

—*Mary Pipher*

Stories are a powerful and often underused leadership tool that can evoke emotions, alter understanding of important issues, and cause educators to think about issues or problems in new ways. When used as a supplement to abstract presentations of research and professional literature, well-chosen stories overcome listeners' natural tendency to judge and debate the speaker's viewpoint. Such stories allow listeners to gain empathy by learning about someone else's experiences, provide concrete experiences to create shared understanding, and evoke positive emotions that motivate action.

. . . .

Today I will be alert for events I can relate to others as stories that will motivate, uplift, or offer guidance to the school community.

120

Use Every Opportunity to Promote Learning-Oriented Conversations

> If you advocate with the intention to persuade, control, or manipulate others, the group will instantly fall out of dialogue. Advocacy spoken with the attitude that "I am right" squashes listening and triggers defensiveness, aggression, and/or withdrawal. In such advocacy, there is no invitation to hear and learn from differing perspectives.
>
> —*Linda Ellinor & Glenna Gerard*

The most effective leaders in continuously improving teaching, learning, and relationships in schools maximize conversations to promote professional learning and minimize advocacy, debate, and compliance-oriented directives. These leaders see themselves as teachers who use learning through conversation as a fundamental means of achieving important goals. They promote interactions in which participants respectfully share their viewpoints regarding important issues and carefully listen to each other with openness to learning through an exchange of perspectives.

. . . .

Today I will look for opportunities to promote meaningful learning through conversation rather than by disseminating information, issuing directives, or advocating a viewpoint.

121

Develop Clarity Regarding Professional Learning

> Team learning is vital because teams, not individuals, are the fundamental learning units in modern organizations.
>
> *—Peter Senge*

Team-based professional learning is a primary means by which school communities achieve their most important instructional goals. The purpose of such learning is the development of new beliefs, a deeper understanding of important ideas, and the acquisition of new practices, all in the service of student learning. Effective leaders believe that effective teams both tap and develop the talents of their members, and that while carefully chosen consultants, courses, and conferences can enrich and support team-based learning, they can never replace it.

. . . .

Today I will assess the extent to which team-based learning is a core feature of our improvement efforts and determine a next step for strengthening it through professional reading or conversations with colleagues.

I22

Develop Discernment Through Solitude and Community

> Every person is grounded with an inner source of truth. . . . Our inner life
> of mind and spirit is interrelated with our outer life of action and service.
>
> —*Thomas Beech*

Leaders possess deep, sustaining parts of themselves that provide compelling purposes for their work and are the ultimate source of their identity, integrity, and vitality. Solitude and reflective writing are common means by which leaders can access the "small, still voices" that often are unheard in the clamor and frenetic pace of their daily work lives. When such "inside" truths are examined and tested "outside" in a sustained community, leaders' discernment and clarity regarding important issues grows.

· ·

Today I will use a period of solitude or journaling to quiet my mind so that I better understand what my "inner teacher" feels about a subject of importance to the school community. At the first available opportunity, I will share with others the perspectives I have gleaned from that experience in the spirit of mutual learning and influence.

123

Learn in Community While Solving Real Problems

> We learn with others. . . . Our ability to make sense of the realities we face, to interact successfully with our environment, to learn from our experiences, is derived from collaboration and collective problem finding and solving.
>
> —*Giselle Martin-Kniep*

Significant professional learning and improvement is often motivated by or is a byproduct of school communities identifying significant problems and collaboratively seeking effective ways to solve them. Professional learning is strengthened when closely connected to the "doing" of school improvement and is periodically reflected on as part of the problem-solving process. Collaborative problem solving that is motivated by worthy goals produces important learning and assists the school community in identifying additional areas in which new learning is essential.

• •

Today I will ask one or more of my colleagues to reflect on the learning that occurred for them while solving important problems with others and to consider how that learning could be applied in future situations.

124

Cultivate Professional Literacy

Generous amounts of close purposeful reading, rereading, writing, and talking, as underemphasized as they are in K–12 education, are the essence of authentic literacy. These simple activities are the foundation for a trained, powerful mind. . . .

—*Mike Schmoker*

Effective leaders make their own learning a professional priority. They take the time to read, to reflect on their experiences through writing, and to listen carefully to the views of others. Just as they desire to cultivate literacy among K–12 students, successful leaders take the time—even just a few minutes a day—to cultivate their own professional literacy and that of others for the benefit of all their students.

Today I will spend a few minutes carefully reading an article or part of a book that is important to the work of the school community. I will respond actively to what I read by making comparisons with what I already know and believe and by raising new questions for exploration.

125

Choose Growth Over Atrophy

> The premise behind incremental change is that the basic structures are sound but need improving to remove defects.... Fundamental changes, on the other hand, are those that aim to transform and alter permanently those very same structures.
>
> —*Larry Cuban*

Organizations either grow or atrophy. Leaders promote continuous improvement when they assist school communities in establishing compelling and transformative visions for their collective future that require substantial changes—what some call *deep change*—in structures, roles, processes, and, most importantly, in the beliefs, understandings, and practices of community members. Deep change counteracts the naturally occurring forces of decline that operate in all organizations and dramatically increases the likelihood that improvements in teaching and learning are sustained rather than dissipated when a leader moves on or project funding ends.

. . . .

Today I will stimulate sustained organizational growth by aligning my beliefs, words, and actions with the achievement of the school's vision of its future.

126

"Reinvent" Yourself

Few people are good at reinventing themselves. They often choose the destructive alternative of staying very busy. It may not be effective behavior, but it has the effect of a good narcotic.

—*Robert Quinn*

Fundamental change in organizations often requires that leaders "reinvent" themselves in ways that take them out of their comfort zones. While reinvention may sound like a radical transformation of personality, it can often be accomplished by relatively small but well-targeted changes in habits of mind and practice that produce profound results over time. To that end, leaders must surrender their addiction to the fast-paced activities that impede focus on the development of new habits.

. . . .

Today I will retreat from my busyness to focus on the development of one or two habits that will make the largest improvements in my ability to serve the school community.

127

Promote Civility

A human moment occurs anytime two or more people are together, paying attention to one another.

—*Edward Hallowell*

High-performance cultures are built on relationships that are caring, sensitive, considerate, and mutually respectful. Leaders of civil communities are aware of the effects their actions have on others and how those effects can ripple throughout the school community. Consequently, they intentionally cultivate positive interpersonal habits within the community, beginning with themselves.

. . . .

Today I will be consciously be aware of the effects my words and actions have on others. When my words and actions have an unintended negative effect, I will remedy the situation as soon as possible.

128

Listen With Empathy

When we move out of ourselves and into the other person's experience, seeing the world with that person, as if we were that person, we are practicing empathy.

—*Arthur Ciaramicoli & Katherine Ketcham*

Leaders who consistently display empathy regarding the experiences and perspectives of others strengthen relationships and cultivate a reservoir of good will. Empathic leaders fully and deeply hear what others say, convey both verbally and nonverbally that they understand that person's perspective, and demonstrate respect for the speaker's viewpoint without necessarily agreeing with it. Through their words and demeanor, these leaders communicate that they value both the message and the messenger.

. . . .

Today I will demonstrate through my words and demeanor attentive listening and a deep honoring of others' perspectives.

129

Offer Generosity of Spirit

Positive emotions such as compassion, confidence, and generosity have a decidedly constructive effect on neurological functioning, psychological well-being, physical health, and personal relationships.

—*Richard Boyatzis & Annie McKee*

Leaders create positive emotions in the school community when they consistently demonstrate respect for others, speak with kindness, honor others' opinions, and disagree graciously while candidly expressing their views. These leaders offer a generosity of spirit that assumes others are honest, trustworthy, and capable unless strong evidence exists to the contrary. They are intentional and persistent in embodying positive attitudes in their day-to-day interactions with staff members, parents, and students.

• •

Today I will exhibit positive emotions and offer respect and compassion to everyone through my words and actions.

130

Appreciate

I beseech you, by all angels, to hold your peace, and not pollute the morning, to which all the housemates bring serene and pleasant thoughts, by corruption and groans.

—*Ralph Waldo Emerson*

School cultures in which expressions of gratitude, appreciation, and celebration far exceed those of blaming and complaint generate positive energy that sustains continuous improvement efforts. Such cultures have leaders who cultivate gratitude in both their personal and professional lives. These leaders also establish rituals and routines through which others can express gratitude in meetings and other settings (for instance, faculty meetings might begin with expressions of appreciation or celebration regarding the actions of colleagues, students, or parents).

. . . .

Today I will speak with others about things for which I am grateful to increase my own sense of gratitude and will identify a ritual of appreciation and celebration that I can initiate in an ongoing group of which I am a part.

131

Use Language That Promotes Community

"We" is a more powerful word than "I."

—Anonymous

Effective leaders create a sense of "we-ness" regarding both the school community as a whole and subgroups such as departments or grade-level units. While these groups may be given various titles—team and professional learning community are two of the most common—they are based on an underlying belief that "together we can accomplish that which we cannot accomplish alone." To that end, these leaders are far more likely to use the pronouns "we" and "our" than "me" and "mine" when referring to school values and goals.

• • • • • • • • • • • • • • • • • • • •

Today I will monitor my language for its inclusiveness (the use of "we" and "our") to promote a sense of community.

132

Express Your Views

> You can't be too honest in describing big problems, too bold in offering
> big solutions, too humble in dealing with big missteps, too forward in
> retelling your story or too gutsy in speaking the previously unspeakable.
>
> —*Thomas Friedman*

Leaders who are forthright in expressing their views on subjects of importance to the school community are more effective in supporting it in achieving substantial goals. These leaders accurately describe current reality, offer stretching visions for a preferred future, and courageously discuss "undiscussables." While they often assert bold purposes and ideas, they consistently do so in ways that promote professional learning through dialogue to build consensus within the school community.

. . . .

Today I will express rather than withhold my views on matters of substance, doing so in the spirit of civility and dialogue to simultaneously deepen understanding and to encourage others to do the same.

133

Promote a Sense of Efficacy

> The cultures of low-performing schools reflect a learned helplessness. Teachers in these schools "learn" that nothing ever gets better and nothing they do matters, so they hunker down and wait for each new program to pass as quickly as possible. . . . In contrast, teachers in high-performing schools believe that as individuals, and as a group, they are capable of improving student achievement, and they trust their colleagues to work as hard as they do to make it happen.
>
> —*Bryan Goodwin*

Because school cultures are powerful forces in supporting or inhibiting continuous improvement, a fundamental leadership responsibility is the creation of cultures that are trusting and that promote a sense of individual and collective efficacy regarding the achievement of important goals. Through sustained team-based learning, teachers acquire knowledge and skills that enable them to feel competent and confident in improving the achievement of all students. High levels of trust support teachers in having courageous conversations and in sharing both their struggles and successes with one another.

. . . .

Today I will assess whether the culture of the school community leans toward learned helplessness or in the direction of trust and competency. If the culture primarily expresses learned helplessness, I will share my observation with the school community and determine with others the next step we will take to address this problem.

134

Believe That the "Impossible" Can Be Achieved

We can do more than we think we can.

—Kimberly Brown-Whale

Successful school communities continuously extend their sense of what is possible for their students. High levels of learning for all students begins with leaders' heartfelt belief that the "impossible" can be achieved, an authentic hopefulness that spreads throughout the community. This hopefulness, combined with a strong plan that focuses improvement efforts on a small number of learning goals, fuels continuous improvement efforts.

. . . .

Today I will examine my beliefs and attitudes to determine whether they limit the school community's sense of possibility, and I will act to address any shortcomings I may find.

135

Make Choices That Serve the School Community

> You rarely have time for everything you want in this life, so you need to make choices. And hopefully your choices can come from a deep sense of who you are.
>
> —*Fred Rogers*

Effective improvement efforts focus on a small number of areas that research and experience indicate have a disproportionately positive influence on improving teaching, learning, and relationships in schools. To that end, leaders make principle-based and goal-driven choices to advance the school community in the achievement of its most important purposes. Rather than react to events, these leaders use both moral and intellectual compasses to guide them in making decisions that best serve the well-being of students and the broader school community.

• •

Today I will determine one or two of the most important things I can do this day—no matter how small—to advance the school community's mission, and I will persevere in accomplishing those tasks despite predictable and unpredictable obstacles.

136

Articulate Ideas to Deepen Understanding

[U]nless we are required to articulate to others what we think, feel, and believe—and receive timely and appropriate feedback from teachers and peers—most of us convince ourselves that we understand something even when we do not.

—*Richard Hersh*

Learning-oriented leaders regularly articulate the school community's most important values, ideas, and practices both to communicate them and to extend and deepen their own understanding of them. Learners—no matter whether they are five or fifty-five—acquire new understanding and skills when they express to others through various means what they think, feel, and believe. Only through the process of making external that which was previously internal can leaders as learners accurately assess their own progress and make plans for improvement.

. . . .

Today I will deepen my understanding of an important idea by writing or speaking about it. Also, I will seek the perspective of one or more colleagues regarding both the accuracy of my understanding and the clarity of my expression.

137

View Obstacles as Spurs to Creativity

You're not going to get much creativity unless there is some degree of encounter, opposition, and something to bang up against. You don't create in a vacuum.

—*Dean Williams*

Creativity and innovation are fueled rather than restrained by the challenges inherent in all important human endeavors. Creators and innovators in all fields—the arts, business, and education, among others—seek solutions within the existing realities of their fields. Effective leaders enable school communities to view "the givens" as spurs to innovation and improved performance rather than as insurmountable obstacles to progress, a perspective that stimulates higher-order thinking and creative problem solving.

· · · · · · · · · · · · · · · · · · · ·

Today I will make a conscious choice to view the constraints related to a particular problem as opportunities to think more deeply about the situation and to innovate at higher levels.

138

Build Relationships

Command and control can't resolve the complex problems of our time. We need leaders who build alliances, cultivate trust, and create conditions where diverse people can come together to do their best and most inspired work.

—*Sam Intrator & Megan Scribner*

Effective leaders enable and inspire excellence by establishing and strengthening relationships within their schools and throughout the community. They understand that continuous improvements in teaching and learning cannot be mandated, and that teamwork and trust are fundamental sources of energy and expertise that fuel superior performance. These leaders also understand that relationship building requires intention and attention, and consequently make it one of their highest priorities.

. . . .

Today I will identify one or more activities that will enhance relationships within the school community and include them in my daily schedule.

139

Be Clear About Your Purpose

Man's vitality is as great as his intentionality: they are interdependent.
—Paul Tillich

Leaders are more effective in achieving the results they most desire when they are clear and transparent about their purposes and those of the school community and about the methods by which those purposes will be achieved. Clarity of purpose can be developed through reading, writing, and sustained conversation with others to develop deeper understanding. Rather than impose their values, purposes, or ideas on others, leaders offer their clarity to the school community in the spirit of dialogue to produce increasing levels of clarity throughout the organization. In meetings and one-to-one conversations, leaders create consensus regarding goals and a collective understanding of the ideas and practices that improve teaching and learning for all students.

. . . .

Today I will share with someone a concise statement of a purpose or outcome for an important schoolwide issue or event. I will check to determine whether my statement is clearly understood.

140

"Perturb the Organism"

By our willingness to name what is, we can take steps to lovingly perturb the organism, the system, the body politic, in specific and perhaps wise ways . . . ways that may generate new ways of seeing.

—*Jon Kabat-Zinn*

Leaders who candidly and respectfully offer their views regarding current reality through meaningful conversations enable the school community to address important issues. When leaders withhold their views, they become unwitting allies of the status quo. The right words at the right time can "lovingly perturb the organism"—in this case, the school community—to higher levels of accomplishment.

Today I will identify and address with others a topic I have avoided discussing and whose airing is essential in moving the school community forward.

141

Teach to Learn

When you teach, you learn.

—*Helen Suzman*

Successful leaders are teachers who promote their own learning and that of the school community by addressing important values, ideas, and practices. Because teaching is far more than telling or directing, these leaders design experiences through which community members can learn—visits to successful schools with similar student demographics, for instance—and provide opportunities for themselves and others to reflect on the implications of those experiences for the achievement of important goals. They also engage in sustained, courageous conversations in various settings to promote professional learning and to stimulate a continuous stream of goal-focused actions.

• • • • • • • • • • • • • • • • • • • •

Today I will select a value, idea, or practice that is important to the school community and determine how I could best engage others in understanding it more deeply.

142

Assume Responsibility

> How do we get those people to change becomes . . . what is my contri-
> bution to the problem I am concerned with.
>
> *—Peter Block*

Effective leaders seek to understand the unintentional and often unrecognized ways in which they contribute to their most vexing problems. Leaders may unwittingly perpetuate problems by withholding their views in important conversations, by not making requests regarding things that are important to them, or by not promptly addressing unkept agreements. They may also contribute to the maintenance of the status quo (and feel overwhelmed at the same time) by taking on community members' problems rather than expecting the individuals involved to play a significant role in problem solving.

. . . .

Today I will identify an important problem and assume for the moment that I am 100 percent responsible for its continuation to see what insights may arise that will lead to new problem-solving approaches on my part.

143

Acknowledge Your Own Uncertainty

Of all the qualities in a manager conducive to innovation and initiative, a degree of *uncertainty* may be the most powerful. If a manager is confident but uncertain—confident that the job will get done but without being certain of exactly the best way of doing it—employees are likely to have more room to be creative, alert, and self-starting.

—*Ellen Langer*

Skillful leaders blend a sense of possibility about a better future with a recognition that they do not have to have solutions to all the problems that lie ahead. They understand that solutions to significant problems are, to a large degree, invented by the school community and may be unlike those found by other schools. These leaders also understand that inventing their way forward involves learning by doing as the community moves ever closer to its preferred future by carefully considering its next steps, taking action, and reflecting on the consequences of those actions to determine future steps.

. . . .

Today I will find an opportunity to acknowledge that I do not have all the solutions to the school community's most pressing problems and affirm my belief in the school community's ability to invent and learn its way to its preferred future.

144

View Conversations as a Learning Process

All learning is social. It is with our peers that we will ultimately find our voice and change our world. It is in community that our lives are transformed.
—*Peter Block*

Conversations among educators are a vital source of professional learning and continuous improvement in teaching and learning. In learning-oriented conversations, participants practice deep, committed listening and display openness to being influenced by the perspectives of others. While conversations that produce learning usually take place in meetings, they can also occur in relatively brief, informal exchanges in hallways or over a cup of coffee.

. . . .

Today I will take advantage of a brief opportunity to explain to others my viewpoint on an important subject and to solicit their perspectives. I will not necessarily seek agreement, but rather an exchange of views that will enable participants to better understand and learn from one another.

145

See Opportunities in New Realities

It is not the strongest of the species that survives, nor the most intelligent that survives. It is the one that is the most adaptable to change.

—*Charles Darwin*

Effective leaders cultivate discernment regarding situations in which it is important to take a stand based on fundamental values and those in which it is best to adapt to new realities. These leaders consistently act on behalf of core principles while acknowledging the inevitability of changing circumstances. They also seek and take advantage of the opportunities usually found within new realities to further their schools' purposes.

Today I will consider ways in which a change within or around our school can serve as a stimulus for learning and growth.

146

Write Simply

> Writing with simplicity requires courage, for there is a danger that one will be overlooked, dismissed as simpleminded by those with a tenacious belief that impassable prose is a hallmark of intelligence.
>
> —*Alain de Botton*

Clear, crisp writing by leaders is an important means by which others in the school community acquire clarity. Accessible writing is an expression of clear thinking, and leaders' clear thinking about key values, ideas, and practices enhances the clarity and learning of others. Abstract, jargon-filled writing is a barrier to shared understanding and consensus-based planning.

. . . .

Today I will carefully examine the clarity and precision of my writing as both a means of communicating and a way of promoting professional learning.

147

Find Creative Solutions Through Collaboration

Most original thinking comes through collaboration and through the stimulation of other people's ideas.

—*Sir Ken Robinson*

The synergy found within groups is an important source of innovative solutions to complex problems. Creativity is aided when leaders encourage the expression of differing viewpoints and invite members of the school community to hone their thinking by testing it against that of others. Creativity is also aided when individuals build on one another's ideas and experiences.

· · · · · · · · · · · · · · · · · · · ·

Today I will tap the creativity found in collaborative inquiry to seek an innovative solution to a significant problem.

148

Design Meetings for Maximum Engagement

Never Work Harder Than Your Students [book title]

—*Robyn R. Jackson*

Learning at any age requires sustained intellectual effort and emotional engagement on the learner's part. Faculty meetings dominated by leaders' presentations are no more effective in promoting learning than classrooms in which teachers' talk suppresses student engagement. Consequently, leaders carefully design meetings to maximize the engagement of participants based on the learning or decision-making goals of the event.

· ·

Today I will design the agenda of a meeting to produce significant intellectual engagement on the part of all participants. To that end, I will make certain that participant talk far exceeds leader talk.

149

Create Intellectual and Emotional Connections

By engagement, I do not mean simply keeping students busy and interested, but rather expecting them to construct and validate meaning—to make sense of things. Education needs to involve students in a process of purposeful reflection—researching, writing, speaking, and being simultaneously intellectually and emotionally connected with what they are doing.

—Richard Hersh

Leaders who value learning engage teachers in finding personal meaning regarding important values, ideas, and practices through intellectual reflection and emotional connection. Successful leaders understand that continuous improvement is initiated and sustained by both the heart and the head. Consequently, they regularly initiate conversations and activities that promote heart-and-head connections as a core feature of the school culture.

• •

Today I will establish personal meaning regarding an important value, idea, or practice and engage others in finding such meaning for themselves and for the school community.

150

Learn Actively

> There is now a massive amount of evidence from all realms of science that unless individuals take a very active role in what it is that they're studying, unless they learn to ask questions, to do things hands on, to essentially recreate things in their own mind and transform them as is needed, the ideas just disappear.
>
> —*Howard Gardner*

Leaders who stretch themselves through continuous learning stretch the communities they lead. Because learning literally changes the brain, it requires persistent effort and activity on the learner's part, whether the learner is an administrator, teacher, or student. Leaders alter their brains when they expend energy to deliberately develop new habits of mind and behavior through the creation of learning plans and the conscious rehearsal of new habits of mind and behavior until their brains have new "default settings." They also create new neural networks through the kind of sustained intellectual engagement found in the close reading of professional literature, extended writing, and focused conversation.

* * * * * * * * * * * * * * * * * * * *

Today I will engage deeply in a learning task that requires me to grapple with an idea or problem to make sense of it for myself. As part of that process, I will explain orally or in writing the meaning I have extracted through my effort.

151

Combine Research With Professional Judgment

[T]eachers, schools, and districts should conduct their own informal (and formal) studies on how well an instructional strategy works in their particular context—with their students, their grade level, or their subject matter. No strategy is foolproof. No strategy is proven. You have to see how it works in your particular setting.

—Robert J. Marzano

Educational research loses much of its value if applied in mindless, formulaic ways to the complex problems of teaching and learning. Effective leaders appreciate the power of school context in shaping the use of new practices and engage teachers' professional judgment in applying research. Consequently, school communities incorporate informal and formal assessments into their improvement plans to determine whether a new practice is affecting student learning, and they modify the practice when appropriate to achieve the desired outcome.

• • • • • • • • • • • • • • • • • • • •

Today I will clarify my viewpoint on the uses and abuses of educational research to make certain I understand and can clearly explain both its strengths and limitations.

152

Listen to Students' Perspectives

Students are highly knowledgeable about the things that help them learn—teachers who know their material, care for them, have a sense of humor, and never give up on them, for example.

—*Andy Hargreaves & Dennis Shirley*

Students' voices are important but underused tools for improving teaching, learning, and relationships in schools. Wise leaders understand that young people have a unique and important perspective regarding the work of the school community and that students' views can add significant value to improvement-oriented conversations. Consequently, they incorporate students' perspectives into planning and use them as a source of professional learning for teachers and other educators.

· ·

Today I will determine a way to better understand and meaningfully introduce students' perspectives to the school community as a means of improving teaching, learning, and relationships. Methods I may consider include student surveys, videotaped conversations with students about teaching and learning, the use of student panels at faculty meetings or during professional development sessions, or inclusion of one or more students on a school improvement committee.

153

Tap Talents to Achieve Extraordinary Results

Leadership is ultimately about creating a way for people to contribute to making something extraordinary happen.

—Alan Keith

Successful school communities find numerous ways to tap everyone's talents to achieve extraordinary results for students. The process begins when schools establish worthy, stretching goals that inspire the best in community members. It continues when schools identify and use the strengths of students, parents, teachers, and administrators and guide the coordinated application of those talents across many months and years.

. . . .

Today I will consider the extent to which the school community recognizes and taps the talents and leadership abilities of all its members by listing those strengths and reflecting on the ways they are or could be used to achieve important goals.

154

View "Gaping Unknowns" as a Resource

We want progress in medicine to be clear and unequivocal, but of course it rarely is. Every new treatment has gaping unknowns—for both patients and society—and it can be hard to decide what to do about them.

—*Atul Gawande*

Effective leaders use the "gaping unknowns" of educational research to stimulate the invention of continuous improvement efforts appropriate to their school communities. Rather than succumb to cynicism or resignation about the ambiguity of research, these leaders use this ambiguity to stimulate conversations that cultivate professional judgment and promote creative solutions to instructional problems. They use the best evidence they can find to stimulate discussion about assumptions and practices, to determine next steps, and to assess progress.

. . . .

Today I will reflect on my own tolerance for ambiguity in research (and in other aspects of the professional literature) and determine how the research that is available can be used to stimulate substantial conversations about important professional issues.

155

Aim High

The greater danger for most of us is not that our aim is too high and we miss it, but that it is too low and we reach it.

—*Michelangelo*

Effective leaders encourage school communities to aim high to achieve significant goals that benefit all students, goals that initially may seem impossible to realize. These leaders know that even if these stretch goals are not achieved, the progress made because of the deep changes they require will far exceed the results obtained through modest, incremental objectives. They also understand the importance of frequent celebrations to recognize indicators of progress in the achievement of the stretch goal.

• •

Today I will carefully examine an important school goal for the trajectory of its aim—how it embodies high expectations for students and adults alike and benefits all students—and consider ways in which we have or will celebrate milestones of progress.

156

Keep Agreements

When you realize how important your integrity and self-esteem really are, you will stop making casual agreements just to get someone off your back. . . . You will make fewer agreements, and you will do whatever it takes to keep them.

—Jack Canfield

A primary attribute of leaders' integrity is their consistency in keeping their word. Simply put, these leaders match word and deed. To that end, they cultivate their ability to say "no" when appropriate so that they do not overpromise and underdeliver. They also carefully monitor their progress in fulfilling the promises they make, knowing that their integrity is on the line.

. . . .

Today I will thoroughly consider all agreements I am about to make to be certain that I can fulfill their standards and deadlines. If I do not already have one, I will create a written promise-tracking system so that I do not inadvertently lose track of agreements I have made.

157

Slow Down the Pace of Conversations

Most communication resembles a Ping-Pong game in which people are merely preparing to slam their next point across; but pausing to understand differing points of view and associated feelings can turn apparent opponents into true members of the same team.

—*Cliff Durfee*

Leaders who slow down the pace of conversations to listen carefully to others' viewpoints strengthen relationships, stimulate professional learning, and enable genuine teamwork. These leaders understand that creating even a brief period of wait time to absorb the viewpoints of various speakers signals to others that their views are worthy of careful consideration. Important learning often occurs in the "spaces" created by such pauses.

. . . .

Today I will consciously slow down the pace of my interactions with others to fully consider their perspectives before offering my viewpoint. When appropriate, I will ask others to do the same regarding my perspective.

158

Give the Gift of Your Honest Self

The greatest gift you ever give is your honest self.

—Fred Rogers

Leaders' honestly, offered respectfully, is a gift to the school community. While truth telling may provoke tension in both the teller and recipient, it is often an essential first step in creating schools in which both students and adults thrive. And because of their unique perspective, leaders possess a viewpoint unlike that available to any other member of the school community, a perspective that, if absent, would seriously impede sustained improvement efforts.

. . . .

Today I will reflect on a truth available only to me because of my unique position in the school community and find an opportunity to share it with others.

159

Learn Every Day

[S]uccessful leaders take responsibility for their own development and are perpetual learners.

—Pam Robbins & Harvey Alvy

Leaders of high-performance cultures demonstrate through their example both the power and positive effects of professional learning. They stretch themselves by setting ambitious goals for their own performance, and then learn their way into the achievement of those goals. Because the learning of these leaders is transparent, their efforts and the results they achieve are evident to the school community and inspire others to higher levels of performance.

. . . .

Today I will review and refine my professional learning agenda and consider ways I can make visible to the school community its challenges and rewards.

160

Highlight the Positive Differences the School Community Makes

Great teachers and great principals make a tremendous difference in students' lives. . . . They change student lives on a daily basis.

—*Arne Duncan*

Wise leaders continuously remind the school community of the important positive differences it has made and will continue to make in the lives of young people. These leaders use various means to illustrate this point, including stories from their own experiences in the community. They may also ask teachers to share anecdotes regarding differences the school has made and invite former students to provide concrete examples of how the community's influence ripples into the future.

Today I will determine one or more methods through which I can illustrate the specific differences that the school community makes in the lives of young people.

161

Link With Colleagues

[T]eachers aren't the only educators whose work is traditionally character-
ized by isolation. Central office administrators and superintendents seldom
get the chance to interact with peers and collaborate on improvement
strategies. And in the rare instances when they do meet with colleagues,
the focus is usually on something other than instructional improvement.

—*Robert Rothman*

Leaders who overcome the isolation of their roles by intentionally link-
ing with like-minded colleagues establish a source of mutual support and
stimulate important professional learning. Because they understand the
intellectual and emotional costs of professional isolation, they reach out
to others who are both close by and at a distance—either face to face or
through the use of technology—to enhance the quality of their work and
their emotional resilience. Such relationships go well beyond "gripe sessions"
to provide hope and offer concrete strategies for continuous improvement.

. . . .

Today I will identify one or more colleagues as potential sources of
mutual support and learning that will enable continuous improvement in
my work and that of the school community. If such a network already exists,
I will express gratitude to its members for our work together.

162

Keep Your Eyes on the Road Ahead

[Don] Tapscott surveyed 11,000 young people and found that today's youth yearn for and demand participation, deep customization of products and services, collaboration, and an opportunity to contribute to solving local and global problems.

—Monica Martinez

Effective leaders prepare the school community for the kinds of teaching, learning, and other experiences that will prepare young people for an unknown and somewhat unknowable world. These leaders are forward thinking, steadfastly keeping their eyes on the road ahead rather than on the rearview mirror of past practice. They engage the school community in sustained study and conversation regarding the world young people are likely to inherit and the kinds of changes required in schools to prepare them for it.

• •

Today I will pause to clarify my thinking about the larger forces that shape the lives of young people—such as climate change, globalization, and technological advances—and about the processes and experiences that will best prepare students for the challenges and opportunities that lie ahead.

163

Strengthen Relationship Skills

The most effective principals operate from a value system that places a high priority on people and relationships.

—*Gordon Donaldson, George Marnik, Sarah Mackenzie & Richard Ackerman*

Leaders who promote strong, positive relationships within the school community and with external partners extend their organizations' capacity to achieve important goals. To that end, these leaders strengthen their emotional intelligence and promote relationship-skill development among students and adults alike. They do not take the quality of relationships for granted, and they recognize that if relationships are not intentionally nurtured, they will gradually atrophy and negatively affect the school's culture and its work.

· · · · · · · · · · · · · · · · · · · ·

Today I will reflect on the current state of my relationship skills and set a goal for their enhancement through study and practice.

164

Experience Teamwork With Colleagues

[W]ithout firsthand experience collaborating with their peers, how can we expect school leaders to create a collaborative culture for their teachers?

—*Jane L. David*

Leaders who participate in high-functioning teams with their colleagues are more likely to create such teams as a core feature of their school cultures. Creating for others what they have not experienced firsthand for themselves is difficult for leaders, if not impossible. When leaders understand the benefits and challenges of interdependent work, they are more capable and confident in leading such efforts within their own settings.

* * * * * * * * * * * * * * * * * * * *

Today I will assess whether teamwork with my leadership colleagues is a strong feature of my professional life and identify ways to initiate or strengthen it.

165

Be Fully Present for Others

There was once an elderly, despondent woman in a nursing home. She wouldn't speak to anyone or request anything. She merely existed—rocking in her creaky old rocking chair. The old woman didn't have many visitors. But every couple mornings, a concerned young nurse would go into her room. She didn't try to speak or ask questions. She simply pulled up another rocking chair beside the old woman and rocked with her. Weeks later, the old woman finally spoke. "Thank you," she said, "for rocking with me."

—Unknown

Simple human presence has the power to promote well-being and strengthen relationships. Sometimes the most meaningful leadership act is to simply be fully present for others. A smile, a sympathetic ear, or a reassuring touch is often the most effective means of communicating respect and caring. Sometimes it is just "rocking" with others.

• • • • • • • • • • • • • • • • • • • •

Today I will identify a situation in which I can communicate respect and caring through my presence and attention. I will enter it without an agenda or intention to alter the person or situation.

166

Develop New Habits

Your habits determine your outcomes.

—*Jack Canfield*

Leaders' success is determined to a large extent by their habits. While many habits serve the school community's purpose, others do not and can be changed through persistent practice to serve important goals. Leaders' "default" beliefs, ideas, and behaviors have been reinforced through years of repetition. That means that the acquisition of new habits of mind and behavior requires diligent practice and patience until they are as automatic as the default settings they are replacing.

Today I will list one or two habits I intend to develop in the next six months to significantly improve the quality of my work and relationships. I will use my calendar or other means to remind me to practice the new habits and to monitor my progress.

167

Elevate Values and Ideas

Great minds discuss ideas. Average minds discuss events. Small minds discuss people.

—Eleanor Roosevelt

Effective leaders create strong school cultures by elevating conversations about beliefs, values, purposes, and ideas over those focused on personality and faultfinding. In doing so, these leaders enhance energy through positive relationships rather than dissipate it through persistent negativity. School communities that build consensus regarding beliefs, values, purposes, and ideas through conversation minimize resistance when implementing new practices.

• • • • • • • • • • • • • • • • • • • •

Today I will seek opportunities to promote deep conversations regarding beliefs, values, purposes, and ideas.

168

Use Collaboration to Improve Teaching

Quality teaching is not an individual accomplishment; it is the result of a collaborative culture that empowers teachers to team up to improve student learning beyond what any of them can achieve alone.

—*Tom Carroll*

The support and practical assistance teachers can provide one another far exceeds any that leaders can directly offer them. Consequently, successful leaders make the establishment of a collaborative, results-oriented culture one of their highest priorities. They understand, though, that the creation of such a culture—particularly in schools in which teachers have little experience with collaborative work—requires persistence and patience.

. . . .

Today I will determine an action that I can take in the next week or two to nudge the school community in the direction of deeper and more meaningful collaboration.

169

Promote Purpose, Distribute Leadership, and Develop Competence

The three things that make most people happy are purposes, power, and relationships.

—*Andy Hargreaves & Dennis Shirley*

Leaders who make a positive difference establish compelling purposes for the school community, distribute leadership widely to empower others, and develop competence in solving challenging problems through supportive collegial relationships. These leaders understand that compelling purposes focus energy and that important work cannot be accomplished without tapping the varied and complimentary leadership skills distributed throughout the community. They also know that people have a strong desire to perform competently, and they nurture that competence through job-embedded, team-focused professional learning.

• • • • • • • • • • • • • • • • • • • •

Today I will determine an action that I will take in the near future that promotes clarity of purpose, provides meaningful leadership opportunities to others, or increases competency through various forms of professional learning.

170

Design Schools to Personalize Learning and Strengthen Relationships

We're convinced that the traditional designs for schools and schooling are broken. We need innovation that looks beyond refurbishing those designs. We need a new learning culture based on reconstituting the relationship between teachers and learners.

—*Elliot Washor, Charles Mojkowski & Loran Newsom*

Effective leaders use various structures, processes, and programs to design schools that promote high levels of learning and the development of caring, supportive relationships. These leaders use highly regarded design elements such as small schools, student advisories, mentorships, and service learning to create more personalized learning environments. They also modify schedules and calendars to ensure substantial time for teamwork as a consistent feature of teachers' work lives.

• • • • • • • • • • • • • • • • • • • •

Today I will reflect on ways in which school structures, processes, and programs can be modified or strengthened to better serve student learning and improve relationships.

171

Be Nimble to Express True Urgency

> A real sense of urgency is a highly positive and highly focused force.... [T]rue urgency doesn't produce dangerous levels of stress, at least partially because it motivates people to relentlessly look for ways to rid themselves of chores that add little value to their organizations but clog their calendars and slow down needed action.
>
> —*John Kotter*

Effective leaders create a sense of urgency by relentlessly honing in on a small number of highly leveraged areas that will have the largest influence on learning and relationships. Because they understand that genuine urgency requires nimbleness in responding to emerging opportunities, these leaders are equally relentless in freeing themselves from low-impact, calendar-clogging responsibilities that do little to further the school's purposes and are impediments to swiftly executed goal-focused actions. They consistently demonstrate through their words and actions a sense of urgency about improving teaching and learning for the benefit of all the students who are currently in their schools.

• • • • • • • • • • • • • • • • • • •

Today I will carefully examine my calendar to determine whether it contains sufficient "white space" for me to vigorously pursue emerging opportunities that further the school's mission. If it does not, I will identify one or more ways I can create a more open schedule beginning today, if possible.

172

View Negative Feedback as a Gift

Force yourself not to react to negative feedback defensively; instead, discipline yourself to listen reflectively, particularly when you're deeply hurt by what you hear. Part of your discipline will be to expect that potentially useful feedback will hurt badly in the moment you receive it and make no sense; in fact, it will seem downright wrong . . .

—*Barry Jentz*

Negative feedback provides leaders with an opportunity to improve their performance and to strengthen relationships within the school community. Because leaders are often shielded from unpleasant information and truths, growth-oriented leaders understand that such information is essential in keeping them and the school community on track in achieving important goals. While such feedback is almost always difficult to hear, these leaders view it as a gift and an opportunity for individual and collective development.

• •

Today I will look deeply into myself to determine how open I am to receiving negative feedback and whether my verbal and nonverbal behavior in such situations deprives me of important and useful information. When I receive negative feedback, I will consider ways I can use it strengthen my leadership.

173

Tend to Your Long-Term Personal Health and Emotional Well-Being

[R]esilient leaders look beyond the short term. They know that the long-term health of an organization depends, in large part, on the health of its leaders.

—*Jerry L. Patterson & Janice H. Patterson*

Leaders' physical and emotional well-being determine whether they have the energy and resilience required to sustain the demanding work of continuous improvement over many months and years. To that end, wise leaders develop the long-term habits of eating well, engaging in regular exercise, and getting sufficient sleep to promote a steady flow of energy throughout the day. They also take care of themselves emotionally by ensuring regular periods of quality time with family and friends, participating in engaging hobbies, and taking restorative vacations.

. . . .

Today I will take an action, no matter how small, to nurture my physical health and emotional well-being.

174

Be an Effective Teacher

The most effective leaders ... demonstrate the characteristics of strong teachers: clarity in expectations, belief in the good intentions of those with whom they work, the patience to allow others to learn to "do it themselves," and the humility to give others the credit for accomplishment.

—Susan Graham

Leaders promote professional learning and cohesion among community members when they view the school community as their classroom. Like good teachers, learning-oriented leaders bring clarity of purpose and high expectations to faculty meetings, one-to-one conversations, and other venues. They consistently promote professional learning by designing experiences that offer new perspectives and promote deep reflection on important issues.

• • • • • • • • • • • • • • • • • • • •

Today I will create a "learning plan" for an upcoming meeting that promotes deep understanding and collaboration among members of the school community. To strengthen the learning design, I will invite one or two others to participate in either its creation or its review.

175

Build Community Through Storytelling

Humans are not ideally set up to understand logic; they are ideally set up to understand stories.

—Roger Schank

Stories have the power to build community and effect significant, lasting changes that "rational" discussions do not. Stories can illustrate moral purposes, evoke emotions that fuel long-term commitment, and provide concrete details that give meaning to abstract mission statements. Leaders who constantly scan the school community for real-life anecdotes equip themselves with a tool that enables them to touch hearts, nurture group cohesion, and sustain a sense a purpose amid powerful distracting forces. These leaders encourage others to share their stories as well.

· ·

Today I will invite others in the school community to share stories that illustrate the community's values and purposes, and I will consider ways I can make storytelling a regular feature of various meetings and events.

176

Develop Moral Purpose

The hunger for leadership is at its core a hunger for moral commitment—
for leadership that serves the common good in contrast to personal gain
or aggrandizement alone.

—*Sharon Daloz Parks*

Effective leaders develop the school community's moral purpose through consensus-building dialogue and disciplined daily actions intentionally aligned with that purpose. These leaders understand that community members are motivated by compelling purposes and feel pride in being involved in worthy activities that transcend self. They remind the community of that purpose through storytelling and the use of various symbols and ceremonies that underscore the importance of their collective work.

. . . .

Today I will examine the clarity of my moral purpose and that of the school community and identify ways we can keep it fresh and meaningful over time.

177

See Possibility in the Unexpected

The afternoon knows what the morning never suspected.
—*Swedish proverb*

Wise leaders accept and even thrive on the unexpected, appreciating that unpredictability is a constant feature of work in complex human organizations. While school leadership often requires "going with the flow," that orientation is most effective when leaders are ever mindful of the school community's values and overarching goals and look for opportunities to further those purposes. As a result, they see possibility in the unexpected rather than allow themselves to be distracted from their priorities by an artificial sense of urgency.

. . . .

Today I will look for ways I can use the unanticipated to reinforce the purposes and values of the school community.

178

Dream Big Dreams

> It doesn't take any more energy to create a big dream than it does to create a little one.
>
> —*Wesley Clark*

Leaders who nurture the individual and collective dreams of the school community stimulate a sense of possibility and create energy for the realization of those dreams. Even if schools fall short of attaining the stretching goals contained in those dreams, their achievements will still far exceed those produced by more modest ambitions. To maintain focus and energy over the many months and years required to achieve such outcomes, leaders make certain the community regularly celebrates milestones en route to the larger purpose.

. . . .

Today I will capture my dream for the school community in writing and share it with others to stimulate a new and larger sense of possibility for the community's collective future.

179

Learn to Say "No"

[H]ighly successful people say no all the time—to projects, to crazy deadlines, to questionable priorities, and to other people's crises.

—*Jack Canfield*

Leaders who succeed in focusing their energy and that of the school community on things that are truly important have learned to say "no" to many less consequential activities. While saying "no" may be difficult at times, wise leaders understand that their organizations' success in achieving their goals depends on their ability to do so. They view every "no" as a teachable moment to reinforce the importance of an unrelenting focus on the school community's overarching purposes.

. . . .

Today I will reflect on my ability to say "no" to distracting meetings and tasks that do little or nothing to further the school community's primary goals. I understand that sometimes saying "no" will be difficult, if not impossible, but for the good of the school community I will persist in becoming more skillful and courageous.

180

Commit to a Small Number of Professional Learning Goals

> With time and thought, anyone can generate dozens of ideas from this book that are relevant to a specific situation. My advice: don't try. A long list can be overwhelming. . . . A better strategy is to identify three or four ideas that will be easy to implement, and start doing so immediately.
>
> —*John Kotter*

Effective leaders make distinctions in degrees of importance among many worthy activities. That is as true regarding the application of new professional learning as it is in other areas. Because these leaders understand that they have neither the time nor energy to deeply understand and practice every possible skill, they select a small number of areas for extended study and application.

· ·

Today I will select a small number of learning goals and commit myself to practicing new behaviors regularly in upcoming weeks and months until they become habitual. I also will use my calendar to remind me to monitor both my skillfulness in their application and their effectiveness in achieving the results I most desire.

Epilogue

You have completed your journey through 180 meditations on various subjects germane to school leadership. You may have read them sequentially, dipped into them based on your interest that day, or selected several meditations on a particular theme for deeper consideration.

Sequential readers began with Robert Quinn's admonition that "successful leadership is continuous personal change" that leads to "inner growth and empowerment" and that "empowered leaders are the only ones who can induce real change." They concluded with John Kotter's recommendation that books such as this one be used "to identify three or four ideas that will be easy to implement, and start doing so immediately."

Thorough readers have circled back on several critically important topics a number of times—purposefulness, clarity, stretch goals, school culture, teamwork, integrity, hopefulness, and storytelling, among others—to experience them from a slightly different angle and to ponder various actions they might take to manifest those qualities in their professional lives.

These meditations are intended in part to affect the mental frames through which you view school leadership, because a shift in your viewpoint often leads to profound changes in practice. However, what matters most, of course, is what you do with these ideas—the behaviors you change and the habits you develop. To continue extending and deepening your understanding of these and other leadership-related issues, read my blog at http://dennissparks.wordpress.com.

I look forward to hearing from you regarding the uses to which you have put these meditations and the influence they have on your work and the success of the school community in achieving its most important goals. I can be reached at dennis.sparks@comcast.net.

Author Index

A Leader's Companion
Robert Eaker, Rebecca DuFour, Richard DuFour
Treat yourself to daily moments of reflection with inspirational quotes collected from a decade of work by renowned PLC experts.
BKF227

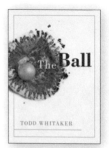

The Ball
Todd Whitaker
Using his gift of storytelling, the author helps you confront critical questions and prioritize your life to stay on your authentic track.
BKN001

On Common Ground
Edited by Richard DuFour, Robert Eaker, and Rebecca DuFour
Examine a colorful cross-section of educators' experiences with PLC. This collection of insights from practitioners throughout North America highlights the benefits of PLC.
BKF180

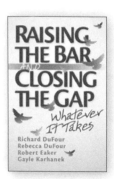

Raising the Bar and Closing the Gap
Richard DuFour, Rebecca DuFour, Robert Eaker, and Gayle Karhanek
This sequel to the best-selling *Whatever It Takes: How Professional Learning Communities Respond When Kids Don't Learn* expands on original ideas and presses further with new insights.
BKF378

Solution Tree | Press
a division of
Solution Tree

Visit solution-tree.com or call 800.733.6786 to order.